Love God's Way

"Two hearts, one faith, a lifetime of love."

Blue Kendria

Copyright © 2025 by **Blue Kendria Berry**

All rights reserved.

No part of this publication may be reproduced in whole or in part, or stored in a retrieval system, or transmitted in any form or by any means, electronic, mechanical, photocopying, recording, or otherwise, without written permission and consent of the publisher, except brief quotes used in reviews.

Scripture quotations are taken from the World English Bible (WEB) and are used by permission (CC0). The World English Bible is in the public domain. For more information, visit https://worldenglish.bible/.

This book is a work of fiction. Names, characters, places, and incidents either are products of the author's imagination or are used fictitiously. Any resemblance to actual events or locales or persons living or dead is entirely coincidental.

Printed in the United States of America

Second Edition, 2025

PAPERBACK ISBN: 979-8-3492-5381-2

HARDBACK ISBN: 979-8-3492-5384-3

EBOOK ISBN: 979-8-3492-5382-9

Red Pen Edits and Consulting

www.redpeneditsllc.com

First and foremost, I want to thank God for His unfailing love and incredible ability to work through me. Without Him, this journey would not have been possible.

I lovingly dedicate this book to my beautiful daughter Shakieria Latunja Dany'qua—my baby cakes—whose smile, presence, and push inspire me every day. To my parents Mitchell and Peggy and sisters Kamilah and Tenisha, thank you for your unwavering love and support. To those dear friends who have been like family, always cheering me on and pushing me to pursue this dream, I love you all to life.

To everyone who played a role in making this book a reality— thank you.

TABLE OF CONTENTS

Chapter 1 1

Chapter 2 12

Chapter 3 20

Chapter 4 31

Chapter 5 41

Chapter 6 48

Chapter 7 59

Chapter 8 71

Chapter 9 76

Chapter 10 85

Chapter 11 100

Chapter 12 120

Chapter 13 126

About The Author 138

CHAPTER 1

It was a beautifully warm afternoon in July. She was pretty busy with work but decided to take a break and go get her some lunch at her favorite wing spot. She walked into Jazzy's Lounge with a slight smile on her face, her mind replaying the amazing time she'd had in morning prayer. It had been a peaceful moment with God, and as she thought about the conversation she had shared with Him, she couldn't help but feel overwhelmed with joy. God was truly answering her prayers, and she was in awe of how faithful He had been.

She made her way to the bar and sat on the stool, waiting for the young lady to come over.

"Yes, ma'am, how may I help you?" The waitress greeted her with a bright smile.

"I'm here to pick up a call-in order," she replied.

The waitress nodded. "The phone number for the order?"

She handed her a card with her number on it. She had previously made the mistake of saying her phone number out loud once before, which resulted in her receiving multiple strange phone calls. After that, she had learned to keep her personal number discreet.

"To confirm your order, 12 of our 24-karat gold wings, all flats with fried okra?" the waitress asked.

"Yes," she confirmed, nodding.

"One moment," the waitress said, walking past her to the kitchen.

Lost in thought, she never noticed the eyes that were on her. The man to her right was staring at her, his gaze intense, but she didn't notice. She was lost in her thoughts, in awe of the things God had spoken to her that morning. She could feel the weight of her prayers being answered, and she smiled to herself, grateful.

"Hi," a voice interrupted her thoughts.

She turned to her left to find a young man sitting beside her, his eyes curious but guarded.

"Hello," she replied, smiling politely.

"You're deep in thought, I see. What are you thinking about, if you don't mind me asking?" he asked, his tone casual but curious.

"God," she said simply, her eyes lighting up as she spoke.

The man looked taken aback by her directness. There was a brief moment of silence as he processed her response. She noticed the shift in his demeanor but continued.

"He is good all the time, isn't He?" she added with a gentle smile.

The man let out a small chuckle, almost nervously. "Yeah, all the time, He is good," he said, a smirk tugging at his lips.

She looked at him with curiosity in her eyes, her smile still warm. "Do you doubt what you're saying?"

The man paused for a moment, then shook his head. "It's just a saying," he said, shrugging.

She shook her head gently. "Not for me," she replied softly.

He seemed astounded by her sincerity. "I just don't understand the hype," he muttered, his voice laced with confusion and sarcasm.

Her smile never wavered. "The hype? It's not hype. Yeshua died for our sins so that we could have a right to heaven and eternal life. That's not hype, that's love," she said, her voice steady and full of conviction.

The man scoffed, rolling his eyes slightly. "Yeah, I hear you," he muttered, clearly uncomfortable with the conversation. Then he paused, raising an eyebrow. "Wait—Yeshua? Who's that? You don't believe in Jesus?"

She smiled gently and replied confidently, "Yeshua is the Hebrew name for Jesus. It's actually his original name, but in English it is translated to 'Jesus'. I prefer to use his Hebrew name because it feels closer to his origins."

She didn't press him further but continued, her tone gentle. "I pray that one day you get to experience the love God has for you and understand just how amazing He really is."

The man's face twisted into a sneer, his patience wearing thin. "Listen," he said loudly, his voice rising, "I don't want to keep talking about the white man's religion." His words were sharp, a hint of disdain behind them.

She kept her calm, her expression unfazed. "No worries, sir," she said with a soft smile. "Have a blessed day."

She picked up her phone and opened her devotion app, her attention shifting back to the peace of her quiet time with God.

The man, clearly frustrated, glared over at her phone screen, trying to see what had captured her focus. *He must have questions,* she thought to herself. *Or he wouldn't be watching me this intently.* She heard the still quiet voice of God telling her to respond with love. At that moment she remembered the scripture in Jeremiah 31: with love and kindness I draw thee.

He then raised his voice again, loud enough for everyone to hear. "And now she's reading her little Bible app. She's a true holy roller," he said sarcastically, his tone dripping with mockery.

Her smile didn't falter, once more she heard the still small voice tell her to pray for him. She said a quick prayer in her heart for him, asking God to soften his heart and open his eyes to the truth. She knew the words weren't about her, but about his own confusion and skepticism.

The man scoffed, sucked his teeth, and stood up from the stool. He walked off, muttering under his breath.

As she sat there with several eyes on her she prayed to be at peace, the restaurant's noise fading into the background, she felt a sense of peace wash over her. *I did what God asked me to do,* she thought. *I didn't let his words shake my faith. I showed him love, and I prayed for him.*

She took a deep breath, the smile still on her face, and waited for her order.

But now, thinking how just a year ago she would have been drawn into an argument, she felt nothing but peace. She smiled softly, shaking her head in amazement at how much God had worked on her heart.

It wasn't that she didn't feel the sting of offense sometimes or that disagreements didn't bother her, but the difference was in her response. Instead of snapping back, she paused, prayed, and remembered that God had called her to be a light, even when it was hard.

"Thank You, Lord," she whispered, her hands resting in her lap. "Thank You for changing my heart. For teaching me to choose love and peace over anger and pride."

She thought about the woman that tried to argue with her just days ago. Instead of stewing over what the woman had said, she'd prayed for them, asking God to bless them and soften their heart. That moment of prayer had felt like a victory, not for her, but for the work God was doing in her life.

Love glanced at her Bible app, recalling the verse she had meditated on earlier that week: Romans 12:18: *"If it is possible, as much as it is up to you, be at peace with all men"* and also the scripture God dropped in her heart during that moment Jeremiah 31:3: *'With love and kindness have I drawn thee."*

It wasn't always easy, but it was worth it. The peace she felt now—the kind that could only come from God—was worth more than any momentary satisfaction she'd once found in "winning" an argument.

God had replaced her need to fight with a desire to love. He'd shown her that peace wasn't just the absence of conflict; it was the presence of His Spirit guiding her to respond with grace, even in difficult situations.

And the best part? That peace wasn't just for her. It was a gift she could extend to others, a way of reflecting His love and grace to the world.

Still meditating on the scriptures in Romans and Jeremiah, the waitress brought her meal to the table. She smiled warmly and handed over her debit card.

"Thank you," she said, her tone gentle.

The waitress smiled, nodded and headed to the register. While Love waited, she noticed a gentleman on the far-right side of the bar watching her. He was tall, dressed casually but neatly, with an air of quiet confidence. When their eyes met, she smiled politely. He returned the gesture, nodding slightly in acknowledgment.

Feeling a bit bashful, she looked away, her cheeks warming. When her card was returned, she thanked the waitress, signed the receipt, and left a generous cash tip. Gathering her belongings, she slid off the stool and began walking toward the exit.

As she got halfway to the door, the man she had previously encountered earlier—the one who'd made a snide comment about her faith—called out.

"Bye-bye, holy roller," he slurred, a mocking, chuckle in his voice.

Her heart began to beat rapidly, but she kept walking, choosing not to engage. *Lord, keep me calm. I don't want my good to be evil spoken of,* she prayed silently.

"Hey!" he called again, his voice growing louder. "You just gonna ignore me?"

"Leave her alone", the waitress called out to him.

She could hear his footsteps behind her, and her pulse quickened. *God, I need you right now.*

When she reached the sidewalk, he caught up and grabbed her arm roughly. "Don't ignore me, super Christian," he spat, his harsh tone laced with sarcasm. "That's not like your God, is it?"

She froze, the sharpness of his grip startling her. Just as she prepared to pull away, a deep, commanding voice cut through the tension.

"Let her go."

Both her and her harasser turned toward the voice. It was the man from the bar—the one on her right who smiled at her earlier. In an instant, he was beside them, his expression calm but firm.

The harasser sneered, loosening his grip and slightly stumbling. "And who are you?"

"The guy who's not going to let you lay hands on a woman," the kind stranger replied. With one swift motion, he grabbed the harasser by the collar and lifted him slightly off his feet. "Leave. Now."

The harasser's voice was shaking. "Okay, okay, I'm going," he mumbled, stumbling backward as the stranger released him.

"Go find something safe to do," the stranger added, his voice steady and unwavering. "Like sleeping off whatever you have been drinking."

The harasser grumbled incoherently and shuffled back into the bar.

She exhaled, her heart racing. "Thank you," she said softly, turning to her rescuer.

He looked at her, his expression softening. "Are you okay?"

"I am now," she replied, offering a small smile.

He nodded, glancing toward the bar to ensure the man hadn't come back. "Let me walk you to your car. Just to be safe."

She hesitated for a moment, then nodded. "Thank you. I'd appreciate that."

She felt a strange mixture of gratitude and curiosity about this man who had stepped in so boldly.

"Well, it seems God put me in the right place at the right time," her rescuer said with a small smile.

She smiled back, feeling a sense of peace settle over her. *Maybe God did,* she thought.

"Are you sure you're okay?" he asked again as they stepped off the curb, concern in his voice as he looked at her.

"Yes, I promise I'm okay. Thank you," she replied, her voice steady but still carrying the lingering effect of the moment. "I really appreciate you."

He nodded. "You're welcome. I was actually coming out to see if I could catch you before you left, and then I saw that he was following you. I'm sorry about him being so rude."

She smiled gratefully with a slight blush creeping across her cheeks. "It's okay, really. But thank you for stepping in." She began to turn to start walking toward her car but then glanced over her shoulder, adding, "My car is right over there, pointing in front of her, you don't have to walk me."

He chuckled and fell into step a few paces behind her. "It's no trouble. I just want to make sure you're safe."

Once they reached her vehicle she turned to face him once more. "This is me. Thanks for walking with me."

"You're welcome," he replied with a smile. "Just wanted to make sure you made it to your vehicle safe." He continued to look at her with a soft, admiring gaze.

She blushed again, feeling the weight of his attention. She cleared her throat, trying to keep things light. "I appreciate your kind gesture. I guess I will get back to work."

The man stuck out his hand. "I'm Troy by the way."

She slowly put her hand in his hand, feeling the warmth of his grasp. "Nice to meet you, Troy, my name is Love."

"Very nice to meet you, Love. Beautiful name for a beautiful woman."

Troy paused, his eyes lighting up. "Love I know this is sudden, but can I take you out some time?"

Love stopped, looking at him curiously. "Did you hear the conversation I had with that guy inside?"

Troy nodded, still smiling. "Yes, I did. And I enjoyed every moment."

"Why did you enjoy that?" she asked, genuinely curious.

"Because I love the passion and love you have for God," he said earnestly. "It did my heart good to see the confidence of God in you. You're not afraid to stand up for your faith, and that's beautiful."

Love's eyebrows twisted in thought, her gaze locked on him. She wasn't sure what to make of his words.

"Were you in there drinking?" she asked, trying to verify if he was worth her time.

"Yes, just an Arnold Palmer with my lunch though," Troy replied with a grin. "You?"

"Oh, you were just there eating lunch?" she said, raising an eyebrow. "I love their wings here. Absolutely the best." She held up her takeout bag, giggling. "Why is it that the best wings always come from the bar or club?"

Troy laughed, shaking his head. "Right? I only come here for lunch. I work across the street and don't have time to go far most days. My office is always busy and someone always needs something, so I come here for a moment of peace and the wings."

"I totally understand that," Love replied.

Troy's expression softened as he looked at her. "So, Ms. Love, may I have your number so that we can plan a date?"

Love raised an eyebrow, surprised at his straightforwardness. "How do you know you'll even like me?"

Troy smiled, a hint of seriousness in his eyes. "From what I have witnessed I already like you now. And I'd like to know you more. I can feel and see the love of God radiating from you."

She chuckled, a little embarrassed. "Wow, laying it on thick, huh?"

Troy's smile faltered slightly, and his tone became more sincere. "I wish you could see what I see."

She looked up at him, her curiosity piqued. "What do you mean by that?"

Troy met her gaze, unwavering. "The Word says you'll know the spirit by the spirit, right?"

She nodded, her heart suddenly beating faster. *Wow a man that knows the word*, she thought. "Yes, it does, she responded."

Troy's voice softened, his sincerity shining through. "I see the fruit, Love. I know we just met however, I'd really like to get to know you more and spend some time with you. I can tell you are someone special, and I don't want to let you slip by."

He handed her his phone, and Love hesitated for a moment before taking it. She quickly dialed her number, once she felt her phone vibrate in her purse she hung up and handed the phone back to him.

"Thank you, Ms. Lovely," Troy said, his smile returning. "I've got to get back to work but enjoy your lunch. I'll talk to you soon, beautiful."

He slowly turned and walked toward his truck, which he realized was parked behind her SUV, he stood beside his truck watching to make sure she was in her vehicle safely. She glanced back at him one last time, giving him a smile. He gave her a smile back that made her heart flutter.

She climbed into her SUV still processing everything that had just happened, started up her SUV, and pulled out of the parking lot, a smile tugging at her lips. She noticed him still standing in the parking lot, watching as she drove away. He stood watching her drive off thinking because he followed the tugging in him today to come here for lunch he may have met his wife. He smiled, got into his truck and headed back to work.

As she drove, her thoughts swirled. *Did he really see all of that in me? Or was it just his way of making conversation?*

But deep down, she knew that whatever it was, there was something different about Troy. And maybe, just maybe, God had orchestrated this encounter for a reason.

CHAPTER 2

Love sat at her desk, organizing her calendar with new appointments and updates that she had received after returning from lunch. Then her phone vibrated against the desk. She reached for it, thinking it was her sister finally responding to set a time to discuss plans for the upcoming holidays which were less than 6 months away.

But to her surprise, it wasn't her sister.

"Troy," she whispered softly, her eyes lingering on his name displayed on the screen. She had saved his number as soon as she got back to her office. A smile spread across her lips, and a flicker of anticipation stirred within her.

Troy: *"Hey Ms. Lovely"*

She felt a surge of excitement seeing Troy's message so soon after they met. She had prayed for a true man of God—someone consistent, who knew what he wanted, wasn't afraid to pursue her, and understood that communication is important.

Love: *"Hello Troy, how are you?"*

Troy: *"I'm great, did you make it back to work okay?"*

Love: *"Yes I did, how about you?"*

Troy: *"Yes, I did. I hope this is not too soon, but I couldn't wait to talk to you."*

Love: She smiled as she typed, her fingers moving swiftly across the screen. *"I'm happy you reached out. Seems like you're somewhat interested in me."*

Troy: *I absolutely am,* he texted back.

Love: *"Most men don't want a truly saved Christian woman,"* she typed, a hint of conviction in her words. *"They're fine with women who talk the talk but don't live it. I live what I speak, and pleasing God is what matters most to me. Yes, I'm human, and I make mistakes, but I don't plan to sin. My walk with God and making it to heaven is my ultimate goal."*

Troy: *"Marry me today,"* he texted jokingly, though there was a hint of seriousness in his text—one only he truly understood.

She paused, a smile tugging at the corners of her lips as she read his words. Although the conversation was lighthearted, something about it felt different, something real.

Troy: She read his message, feeling the weight of his words. He continued, *"But honestly, that's where I am too. My walk with God and living for Him is everything to me. I agree—people don't want to serve God these days. They'd rather chase the pleasures of the world and be destined for hell than honor and follow our Creator, the Almighty God. I've been praying for my wife to come and just waiting on God to bring my Ruth."*

Her heart stirred as she read the sincerity behind his words.

Love smiled softly before typing her response:

Love: *Oh, so you're Boaz?*

Troy's response came quickly.

Troy: *I can assure you, I'm a good man who absolutely loves God, and I will love my wife as Christ loves the church. I'm ready for church worship, praying, Bible study, loving God, cooking together, dancing and cleaning the house, trying new food, bowling, traveling, and enjoying life with my God partner!*

Troy: *And if I may be upfront and honest, speaking it into existence, I believe you are my Proverbs 31 Ruth.*

Love's eyes went wide as she read the last message from Troy. She placed the phone down for a moment, staring off into space. "God, is this You? Have You sent this man? Is Troy my husband, my man of God?" she whispered to herself.

She closed her eyes, listening intently for God's response, but the silence lingered. She knew God's answers often came in more ways than one, and that sometimes His silence didn't mean "no."

She opened her eyes and looked back at her phone, her heart racing with the possibilities.

Troy: *"Blue, are you still there? I hope I didn't scare you off"....*

Love: *"I'm still here"*

Troy: *"I know we just met today, I apologize if that was a turn-off and possibly moving too fast"*

Love: *"No it wasn't. Honestly, I was praying. I consult God in everything for confirmation of his will.*

Love: *"And please don't ever apologize for being a faithful man of God doing what he told you." "Did he tell you to pursue me?"*

Troy: *"That was my confirmation right there. Thank you for sharing that with me. I also prayed about me, you, and us." "His answer was, yes."*

Troy: *"Are you busy tomorrow?"*

Love: *"Just my normal daily devotion and thinking I would go to the museum or drive to the aquarium. Did you have something in mind?"*

Troy: *"Yes I would love to take you to this new place I found."*

Love: *"Okay, where is that?"*

Troy: *"It's a surprise. Now it will take several hours to drive there and back, if that is okay with you?*

Love: *"Wait, you want to spend the entire day with me tomorrow?"*

Troy: *"Yes, I know it's last minute, but I would love to spend the day with you. I know you will enjoy the trip."*

Troy: *"Are you okay if I come to pick you up?"*

She thought for a moment. After a few minutes she responded.

Love: *"Would you be okay if I got back to you with my answer?"*

Troy: *Absolutely, please pray about it and let me know what God says, because I know you're going to the Father,* he typed, chuckling.

Love smiled softly at his words, feeling the warmth of his sincerity. She paused, reflecting on everything that had just been said. Taking some time to go to her heavenly father in prayer and to also reach out to her earthly father.

The phone rang twice before her dad picked up.

"Hello?" her dad answered.

"Hey, Daddy!" she said, her voice light with affection.

"Hey, Babygirl, how are you?" His voice was full of warmth.

"I'm good, Daddy. Do you have a minute to talk?"

"Is everything okay? You don't normally call in the middle of the day like this."

"Yes, sir, everything is good, but I do have some questions."

"Okay, baby girl, what's up?"

"When you met Momma, how soon did you know she was the one?"

Her dad chuckled, recalling the same questions he'd once asked his own father and older brother when he met Love's mother.

"Well, baby girl, I knew the same day that I met your mother that she was going to be my wife. The encounter was brief, but I knew. Your mother is beautiful and has a beautiful voice. She was performing at a jazz club when I met her. I had just come back from my tour in the Vietnam War, and those of us who returned without family nearby all got together and went to the jazz club. There she was, singing her soul to me—at least, that's how it felt. I told my battle buddy that I was going to get her and marry her. I knew right then." His voice softened as he thought back, a proud smile tugging at his lips. "I'm so proud that she's my wife."

"Wow, Daddy, that's beautiful."

"So, about this young man?" her dad asked, his tone shifting slightly.

"Daddy, how—" she started, unsure of how to phrase it.

"I know. You wouldn't be asking me about your mother and me if there wasn't a young man involved. Tell me about him," he said, his curiosity piqued.

She explained what happened at the bar and how he had asked her to spend the day with him the next day.

"Did you pray about it?" her dad asked.

"Not yet. I called you first," she replied.

"Okay, now pray about it. And I say go, if God says the same. You're a great woman of God, and if this man sees that you are the lady he wants to pursue and God says you can trust him, then I trust your decision," her dad responded with confidence.

"Yes, sir. I will pray about it and let you know tonight," she said.

"Okay, baby girl. I'm excited for you. I know your desires and you deserve it all. Everything will work as God has planned."

"Yes, sir. Thank you for talking with me. Love you!"

"Love you more, baby girl. Speak with you later."

They hung up.

For the next few hours, she prayed about the situation in her heart, patiently waiting for God's response. Once she arrived home from work, she took a shower and then settled onto her couch, her Bible in hand.

"Lord, guide me," she whispered as she flipped through the pages without a specific destination in mind. Her hands paused, and her eyes fell on Ecclesiastes 4. She noticed verses 9-12, which she had previously highlighted: *Two are better than one... and a threefold cord is not easily broken.*

She smiled softly, her heart stirring as she continued reading the cross-referenced scriptures: Genesis 2:18 about companionship, Ephesians 5:25-33 on love and sacrifice, Proverbs 18:22 about finding a wife, and 1 Corinthians 13:4-8 on the characteristics of love. Finally, she reflected on Galatians 5:22-23, which detailed the fruit of the Spirit.

As she absorbed the Word, she remembered Troy's words: *"I see your fruit."* Through these scriptures, she felt her answer. Peace and assurance washed over her, and she quietly thanked God for His guidance.

She picked up her phone to reach out to Troy, when it vibrated in her hand. A message notification lit up the screen—it was from him.

She smiled, her heart full of joy, feeling confirmation in the timing.

Troy: *Love, I hope I'm not interrupting you. I've been thinking about you and wanted to see if you received an answer from God.*

Love: *Yes, your timing is perfect. I just received my answer while reading His Word. I will spend the day with you, Troy, and I'm looking forward to it.*

Troy: *Awesome! I'm excited about tomorrow.*

Love: *What time should I be ready?*

Troy: *Actually, I was going to ask you what time I should be there so you can do your devotion—or would you like us to do the devotion together during the ride? It's about a five-hour drive to the place I want to take you.*

Love: *Yes, that sounds awesome. I'd love for us to do the devotion together.*

Troy: *Absolutely. In that case, I'll be at your place by 5 a.m. if that's okay.*

Love: *Yes, I'll be ready.*

About five minutes later...

Troy: *Beautiful, can I get your address?*

Love: *Ohhh, that would be good, so you know where to come, huh? Lol.*

Troy: *Unless you've changed your mind. Lol.*

Love: *No, I haven't at all.*

Troy: *Okay, great to hear. I'll let you get your rest and see you in the morning.*

Love: *One more thing, how should I dress for the trip?*

Troy: *Dress comfortably.*

Love: *Okay. See you in the morning.*

Troy: *Goodnight, see you in the morning.*

CHAPTER 3

The next morning, Love woke up at 4 a.m.—her usual prayer time. It was still dark, and she closed her eyes, letting the quiet settle around her as she prepared her heart to speak with God and get ready for the day. She was grateful for this day, but even more, for the presence of Troy in her life. A man who loved God and wanted to lead her in devotion. It felt like an answered prayer, but part of her hesitated, wary of moving too quickly. She didn't want to assume anything, nor did she want to let fear cloud the blessings God might have for her.

"Lord, you know my heart," she began, her voice soft in the silence. *"You know what I've been asking for all these years. Please give me confirmation that this man is truly from you, that this is your will."* She took a deep breath, releasing her worry. *"I know I heard yes in my spirit yesterday, but I'm asking again because...well, you know me, Lord. You know I tend to overthink. I don't want to mess this up."*

After a moment, she reached for her Bible, flipping it open as she so often did, trusting that God would guide her to what she needed to read. Her eyes fell on Mark 10:9: *"Therefore what God has joined together, let no one separate."*

Love's heart swelled with emotion, and she couldn't help but smile. This verse felt like a gentle whisper from God, a promise that only He could give. It was confirmation in the clearest, most personal way.

"Thank you, Lord," she whispered, closing her eyes and letting the peace wash over her. *"Thank you for answering me so quickly."*

In that moment, Love felt her spirit calm and her doubts fade. She felt ready to embrace this new chapter, trusting that whatever lay ahead, God was guiding her every step of the way. After reading Mark 10:9, Love sat quietly, letting the words sink in. She felt a warmth in her chest, like God was wrapping her in His reassurance. She grabbed her journal and began to write:

"Lord, thank You for speaking to me this morning. Thank You for Troy, for this new connection that feels so different from anything I've known before. I surrender my fears and doubts to You. If this is Your will, please give us both the wisdom and patience to build something that honors You. Let Your love guide our steps."

She paused, tapping the pen against her lips. The thought of Troy leading them in devotion today filled her with anticipation and a little nervousness. She wasn't used to men taking the spiritual lead—it was something she'd prayed for but had rarely seen in her relationships.

Flipping through her Bible, she landed on Proverbs 16:3: *"Commit to the Lord whatever you do, and He will establish your plans."*

The verse brought a sense of clarity. This wasn't about rushing or forcing anything. It was about committing everything—her heart, her hopes, her worries—to God and letting Him guide her steps.

She wrote the verse down in her journal and added a simple prayer:

"Lord, help us to commit this relationship to You, whether it's for a season or for a lifetime. Let Your will be done."

Love set her journal aside and played her favorite worship song, "Goodness of God." As the lyrics filled the room, she lifted her hands, surrendering her day to Him.

When the song ended, she looked at the clock. It was nearly time for Troy to arrive. She showered and got dressed.

As she got dressed, she whispered one last prayer: *"Father, let today be filled with Your presence. Teach us to love You more and to love each other as You would have us. Amen."*

With a smile and a heart full of peace, Love smoothed her dress, grabbed her bag and headed downstairs to wait for Troy, confident that God was in control.

******

Troy woke up well before the sun, his alarm softly playing the hymn *"Great Is Thy Faithfulness."* He stretched, letting the familiar melody remind him of how God's faithfulness and mercies are fresh every morning. He reached for his phone and queued up his worship playlist, filling the room with songs of praise as he moved through his morning routine.

As he brushed his teeth, he caught himself smiling in the mirror. *Today's the day,* he thought, his heart fluttering. It wasn't just any day—it was his first real date with Love. Her name alone made him grin, a subtle reminder of God's promises in every interaction they'd shared so far.

After a quick shower, Troy pulled out the outfit he'd carefully planned the night before—a crisp button-up shirt and dark jeans. He wanted to look his best without seeming overdone. Glancing at his watch, he realized he had extra time. He grabbed his Bible, settled into his favorite chair by the window, and opened to Proverbs 3:5-6:

"Trust in the Lord with all your heart and lean not on your own understanding; in all your ways submit to him, and he will make your paths straight."

He prayed, asking God to guide their day, help him be a man of faith and integrity, and bless whatever the future held for them.

When it was time to leave, Troy grabbed his keys and his overnight bag, his nerves mingling with excitement. As he stepped out the door, he whispered, "Okay, God. Let's do this."

Troy pulled into Love's driveway right on time, his truck freshly washed and stocked with snacks, bottled water, and a playlist he'd curated for the trip. As he stepped out of the truck to meet her, Love walked out, carrying a small overnight bag and wearing a bright smile. Even in the dark he could see how beautiful she was. She wore a royal blue sundress, simple yet radiant, and her shoulder-length sister locks framed her face perfectly. It was early morning but a wonderfully warm Saturday in July.

"Good morning, Troy," she said, her voice cheerful.

"Good morning, Love," he replied, reaching down to give her a warm embrace, then taking her bag and placing it carefully in the backseat next to his. "Ready for a road trip?"

"Absolutely. I even made a list of fun car games and questions to keep us entertained," she said, laughing.

As they settled into the car, Troy turned to her. "Before we start, would you mind if we pray for the trip?"

"Not at all. I'd love that," she said, bowing her head.

Troy grabbed her hands and began to pray he prayed for safe travels, a blessed time together, and that their hearts would be open to what God wanted to show them during the trip and that every place that they go that God will be with them and keep them safe and have victory in him.

The drive began with scripture devotion, moving to easy discussion about the devotion she read as he drove then on to lighthearted topics like their favorite foods, childhood memories, enjoyable activities and even embarrassing moments. They laughed as Love recounted a time, she accidentally sang off-key during a church solo, and Troy confessed to once getting locked out of his house in his pajamas during a rainstorm.

Around the second hour as the sun began to rise, painting the horizon with shades of orange, pink, blue and red and they got closer to their destination the playlist shifted to softer worship songs. The long drive was passing quickly, filled with laughter, shared stories, a deepening sense of connection, and their conversation grew deeper.

"So, what inspired your faith journey?" Love asked, glancing at him as he drove.

Troy thought for a moment, his fingers tapping the steering wheel lightly. "I'd say my parents laid the foundation, but it became real for me in college. There was a time when I struggled with direction—questioning if I was truly living for God or just going through the motions. One night after almost losing my life hanging with the wrong people I just broke down and surrendered everything to Him being so very thankful that I was still living. It was like…a weight I didn't even know I was carrying was lifted off."

Love nodded; her gaze thoughtful. "I've had moments like that too. It's amazing how God meets us exactly where we are."

Troy began to exit the highway heading toward a truck stop, he wanted to stop to refuel and grab coffee. He refueled, they grabbed coffee, a breakfast sandwich from the attached cafe and then back on the road not wasting too much time in order to make it to their destination in good time.

Over steaming cups of coffee, they talked about their favorite Bible stories and how those stories shaped their views on love and trust.

By the fourth hour, Love pulled out her list of car games. "Okay, rapid-fire: If you could meet any person from the Bible, who would it be?"

"Paul," Troy said without hesitation. "The guy went through so much but stayed so faithful, and my dad is named after him, he chuckled. What about you?"

"Ruth," Love replied. "Her loyalty and faith in God are so inspiring. Plus, she reminds me that God's plan is always bigger than we can imagine."

As Troy exited the highway with the destination in view he smiled at Love, not too long right, he asked?

She looked up and realized in her line of sight was the bible museum, a place she had on her bucket to travel to because she heard so many stories and read reviews of how awesome it was and how people actually had encounters with God.

"Oh my goodness, thank you for inviting me to come with you," Love said softly as they approached the museum's towering entrance.

"Thank you for trusting me and joining me on this trip," Troy replied, his heart full.

******

As Love and Troy stepped out of the truck and into the warm yet comfortable air, they exchanged smiles that mirrored their excitement. The towering structure of the Bible Museum stood before them; its architecture as awe-inspiring as the treasures it held within.

Once inside, they were greeted by warm lighting and walls adorned with scriptural art and artifacts. Troy glanced at Love and noticed her wide-eyed wonder as she took in the grandeur of the space.

"Where should we start?" Troy asked, his voice full of anticipation.

Love scanned the directory. "How about the section on the history of Biblical manuscripts? I've always been fascinated by how God preserved His Word through centuries."

Troy nodded. "Sounds good to me. Lead the way."

As they walked through the exhibit, they marveled at ancient scrolls, fragments of frankincense and myrrh, and intricately illuminated manuscripts. Love lingered over a display of a preserved Torah scroll, her fingers brushing lightly over the glass case.

"This is incredible," she murmured. "To think that these texts have been protected for thousands of years... it reminds me of Isaiah 40:8: *'The grass withers, the flower fades, but the word of our God stands forever.'*"

Troy leaned closer, his voice low but full of admiration. "You really know your scripture, don't you?"

Love smiled, a blush creeping up her cheeks. "I want to always keep his words close to my heart.

"Troy smiled impressed. "I feel the same and I can't wait to grow more and more in the word with you!"

They moved on to a section dedicated to the life of Jesus. A large replica of a fishing boat caught Troy's attention, and he pulled Love toward it.

"Look at this," he said, his eyes lighting up. "This must be like the boats the disciples used."

Love stood beside him, taking in the details of the craftsmanship. "I imagine Jesus sitting in one of these, teaching crowds on the shore or calming storms with just a word. It's humbling."

Troy turned to her, his expression thoughtful. "What's your favorite story about Jesus?"

Love didn't hesitate. "The woman at the well. The way Jesus meets her where she is, offering her living water, even when others would have shunned her. It reminds me that God sees us, knows us, and loves us, flaws and all."

Troy nodded, a smile tugging at his lips. "That's a good one. For me, it's Peter walking on water. It's a reminder that as long as I keep my eyes on Jesus, I can do the impossible. But the moment I let fear take over..."

"You start to sink," Love finished, nodding in agreement.

"Exactly," Troy said. "But Jesus is always there, reaching out His hand to pull me back up."

Their conversation flowed naturally as they explored exhibit after exhibit. In the section on Biblical archaeology, they marveled at replicas of ancient cities and artifacts.

Troy stopped in front of a display featuring David and Goliath. "This is one of my favorite stories growing up," he said, gesturing toward the massive spear and sling on display. "It taught me that no matter how small I felt, with God on my side, I could face any giant."

Love grinned. "I can picture little Troy running around pretending to slay giants."

Troy laughed. "Oh, I had a slingshot and everything."

In the interactive section, they both laughed like children as they attempted to build a miniature version of Noah's ark.

"Who knew this would be so complicated?" Troy said, holding up a tiny wooden plank.

"Exactly why Noah needed divine instructions," Love teased, her laughter echoing through the space. She covered her mouth as she noticed others around looking at her.

Toward the end of their visit, they entered a room dedicated to the Psalms. Soft instrumental worship music played in the background, creating a serene atmosphere. Love sat down on one of the benches and closed her eyes, letting the words of Psalm 23 displayed on the wall wash over her heart.

Troy sat beside her, his voice soft. "What's your favorite psalm?"

"Psalm 46," Love replied. "'God is our refuge and strength, a very present help in trouble.' It reminds me to trust Him in every situation."

Troy nodded; his voice equally quiet. "Mine's Psalm 139. 'Lord, you have searched me, and you know me.' It keeps me grounded, knowing He knows me better than I know myself."

They sat in companionable silence for a moment, the weight of God's presence filling the room.

As they exited the museum, the sun was setting, painting the sky with hues of orange and pink.

"This was amazing," Love said, glancing at Troy. "Thank you for inviting me."

Troy smiled. "Thank you for saying yes. I can't remember the last time I had such meaningful conversations and laughed this much in one day."

Love smiled back, feeling her heart swell with gratitude. She didn't know what the future held but today had been a gift—one she would treasure.

Love chuckled. "I agree. And since you brought me here, I have an idea for our next big trip."

"Oh?" Troy asked, raising an eyebrow, his curiosity piqued. "What's that?"

"Have you ever been to the Ark Encounter in Kentucky?" she asked, her face excitedly lit up.

Troy's eyes widened slightly. "You mean the full-scale replica of Noah's Ark? I've read about it, but I've never been."

"Me neither," Love said. "But I've always wanted to go. I heard they have exhibits inside that bring the story of the flood to life, and it's supposed to be incredible."

Troy nodded thoughtfully. "That does sound amazing. I've always been fascinated by the story of Noah—the obedience it took to build the ark, trusting God when the world thought he was crazy."

"Exactly," Love said, her enthusiasm growing. "I think it'd be an incredible experience to see the ark and reflect on the faith it took for Noah to follow God's instructions."

Troy smiled at her, the corners of his eyes crinkling. "You're on, Love. Let's make that our next big trip."

"Really?" she asked, her excitement bubbling over.

"Really," Troy affirmed. "I mean, how could I say no? It's the perfect follow-up to today. Plus, I think it'll be even better exploring it with you."

Love felt warmth spread through her chest at his words. "I'm holding you to that, Troy."

"Deal," he said, offering his hand for a shake.

She took it, laughing softly. "I guess I should start looking at dates, then."

CHAPTER 4

As they exited the museum, the sun was high, painting the sky with hues of red and orange. The day had been a blend of awe, discovery, and heartfelt connection, leaving both of them with smiles they couldn't seem to shake. They didn't realize how quickly the time had passed until they stepped outside, greeted by the soft golden glow of the afternoon sun. Love checked her phone. "Is it 3pm already? Did we really spend most of the day in the museum?"

Troy chuckled, stretching his arms. "I guess time flies when you're diving into God's Word and spending time with great company."

Love smiled. "It was worth it. But I feel like we barely scratched the surface. There's so much to take in."

"We'll definitely have to come back," Troy said. Then, glancing at her with a playful grin, he added, "But only if you come with me again."

"Deal," she said with a laugh. "Now, I don't know about you, but I need to freshen up after all that walking."

"Same here," Troy agreed. "How about we head back to the hotel, take a breather, and then figure out where to eat?"

"Perfect plan," Love said.

As they walked to the car, the conversation turned to what they imagined seeing at the ark and the lessons they hoped to draw from it. Both felt a growing sense of anticipation, not just for the trip itself but for the chance to continue building something special together.

The drive back to the hotel was filled with light conversation about their favorite moments at the museum. Troy teased her about her excitement during the Noah's Ark exhibit.

"You were like a kid in a candy store," he said, grinning.

"I couldn't help it," Love admitted, laughing. "The story of Noah has always inspired me—his faith, his obedience. I mean, building an ark when it had never even rained before? That's next-level trust in God."

Troy nodded. "I can't argue with that. It also shows how God's plans are way bigger than we can imagine. And speaking of Noah, I can't wait for that trip, I'm excited already."

Love's face lit up. "Me too! It's going to be amazing to see it in person."

"I'm ready for our next big trip," Troy said, his grin widening.

Back at the hotel, after they got their key cards, and rode the elevator to floor 7 they parted ways to their respective rooms to freshen up. Love took a moment to reflect on the day as she stood in front of the mirror, smoothing down her locs. She couldn't help but smile, thinking about how effortlessly she and Troy had connected.

After a quick shower and changing into a simple yet chic dress, she checked her phone. A text from Troy popped up:

Ready whenever you are beautiful. No rush.

She smiled and replied: *I'm leaving the room now. Meet you in the lobby.*

When she stepped off the elevator, Troy was waiting for her, leaning casually against a pillar in the hotel lobby. He looked up, his eyes lighting up when he saw her.

"You look amazing," he said, offering his arm.

"Thank you," she said, slipping her hand into the crook of his elbow. "And you clean up pretty well yourself."

"Why, thank you," he said with a mock bow, making her laugh. "So, any ideas on where you'd like to eat?"

"I'm feeling like some hearty and comforting soul food. Thinking like fried chicken, mac and cheese, and greens," she said, grinning.

"Great minds think alike," Troy said, pulling out his phone to search for nearby restaurants. "There's a place called *Georgia Brown's* about ten minutes away. The reviews say their food is so good it's almost heavenly."

"Sold," Love said.

The drive to the restaurant was quick, the sun painting the sky in shades of pink and orange. When they arrived, the savory aroma of fried food greeted them even before they stepped inside.

The warm, elegant interior of *Georgia Brown's* made them feel instantly at home. Scripture verses and inspirational quotes adorned the walls, adding a touch of charm.

After being seated at a small corner table, they scanned the menu.

The server appeared with a warm smile., "Ready to order?"

"Yes", Troy responded, "ladies first he said to Love."

"I think I'll go for the fried chicken, mac and cheese, and candied yams with a lemonade," Love said.

"Shrimp and grits with a glass of cranberry juice for me," Troy replied.

"Awesome I will be back with your drinks", the server replied.

With a playful smirk, Troy looked at Love, "Share your mac and cheese"? "Only if you let me try your grits," Love shot back, making him laugh.

The server returned with their drinks; they ordered croissants to go with their meals and enjoyed each other's company. As they waited, they discussed the ambience and how beautiful the restaurant is with the dimly lit lights and great atmosphere.

Their food arrived, Troy looked at Love, "Can we pray?" "Yes please", she responded. Troy grabbed her hands and began to pray over their meal; *"Lord thank you for this meal let it be a blessing and nourishment to our bodies, bless the hands that prepared the meal and the bellies that will receive and take all impurities out. Thank you for this day and the beautiful companionship of your children, In Jesus Name we pray. Amen"*, they both said simultaneously.

They smiled at each other and began to enjoy their meal. The conversation flowed as naturally as it had all day. They swapped life memories, laughed about family quirks, and shared how life's events have shaped their lives.

"This has been one of the best days I've had in a long time," Love said, her voice soft but full of sincerity.

"Same here," Troy replied, meeting her gaze. "And to think, it's not even over yet."

As they lingered at the table after their meal, they both silently thanked God for the connection they were building—a bond rooted in faith, laughter, and the promise of more to come.

After finishing their meal, neither of them was ready for the day to end. Troy looked at Love as they stepped out of the restaurant. The golden hues of the setting sun bathed everything in a warm glow.

"How about a walk along the boardwalk?" Troy suggested.

Love smiled. "I'd like that."

The soft warm breeze carried the faint scent of the nearby water as they made their way to the boardwalk. The rhythmic sound of waves lapping against the shore created a serene backdrop for their conversation.

They strolled leisurely, talking about everything from childhood memories to how they grew up. Love shared how James 4:7-8 had been her anchor during some of the toughest seasons of her life.

"It reminds me that no matter what, if I resist the devil, he will be with me, that he will be near me if I draw near to him, if I keep praying, keep reading my word, continuously thinking of the good things of God," she said, her voice soft but firm.

Troy nodded; his expression thoughtful. "For me, it's Jeremiah 29:11. It's a constant reminder that God's plans are good, even when life doesn't make sense."

The conversation moved and flowed naturally, each word drawing them closer. As the sun dipped lower on the horizon, painting the sky in fiery oranges and yellow, Troy paused mid-step.

Love turned to look at him. "Everything okay?"

Without a word, Troy reached out and gently took her hand. Love blinked in surprise but didn't pull away. Instead, she felt her heart skip a beat as a quiet warmth spread through her.

Troy met her gaze, his voice soft but steady. "I hope this is okay. I just... I feel like I've known you forever, Love. Like God brought us here for a reason."

Love looked down at their intertwined hands, then back up at him. "It's more than okay," she said, her voice barely above a whisper.

They continued walking, their hands joined, the simple gesture creating a sense of connection neither of them could deny.

The boardwalk was lined with small benches and lights, but they barely noticed, lost in their own little world. At one point, they stopped to lean against the railing, watching the waves dance under the last of the disappearing sunlight.

"You know," Troy said, breaking the comfortable silence, "when I prayed about meeting someone, I never imagined God would answer the way He has."

Love smiled; her eyes fixed on the water. "I prayed, too. For years, actually. And today, it feels like... like a part of those prayers has been answered."

Troy turned to look at her, his gaze filled with admiration and something deeper. "It's amazing how God works, isn't it? Bringing two people together who were praying about it but weren't rushing the moment but still needed it."

Love nodded, meeting his eyes. "His timing is always perfect."

They stood there a while longer, the sound of the waves and the soft murmurs of other boardwalk visitors blending into the background. Finally, Troy spoke again.

"Love, can I pray with you?" he asked.

Love's heart swelled at his words. "I'd love that."

There, on the boardwalk under the hues of evening sky, Troy bowed his head and began to pray aloud. He thanked God for the day, for the experiences they'd shared, and for the connection that was blossoming between them. Love's heart filled with gratitude as she silently prayed alongside him.

When they finished, Troy opened his eyes and smiled at her. "Thank you for trusting me with moments like this."

"Thank you for leading us in moments like this," Love replied.

They continued their walk, the sun having fully set now, leaving the sky sprinkled with stars. As they made their way back to the truck, neither said much, but the peace and joy in their hearts spoke volumes.

As they reached the truck, Troy walked ahead to open the passenger door for Love. She smiled, stepping up onto the side bar she slipped into her seat.

"Thank you," she said, her voice soft.

"Chivalry isn't dead," Troy said with a wink as he closed her door and walked around to the driver's side. Just as he reached for the handle, he noticed the door was already open.

Love had leaned over to open it for him, a small but thoughtful gesture that didn't go unnoticed.

He slid into the seat, glancing at her with a warm smile. "Thank you."

"My pleasure," she replied with a soft laugh.

Troy turned the ignition, and as the car started, he reached for her hand again, gently intertwined his fingers with hers. His voice was low and sincere as he said, "The pleasure is all mine, Love."

She looked down at their joined hands, a smile spreading across her face. There was something about the way he said her name, like it carried weight, like he truly meant it.

They drove in comfortable silence for a few moments, the city lights casting a soft glow inside the car. Love felt a peaceful stillness in her heart, one she hadn't felt in a long time.

Troy broke the silence as they pulled into the hotel parking lot, his thumb lightly brushing against the back of her hand. "You know, I don't think I've ever felt this way so quickly about anyone. There's just... something about you, Love."

Her cheeks flushed, but she met his gaze, her eyes filled with quiet confidence. "I could say the same about you, Troy. But I also know it's not about us. It's about Him, the One who brought us together."

Troy nodded, his grip on her hand tightening just slightly. "You're right. It's amazing how God works. I prayed for someone who loves Him as much as I do, and then... here you are."

Love's heart smiled at his words. She didn't respond right away, instead allowing the moment to settle over them.

Troy turned to her before stepping out. "Today was unforgettable, Love. Thank you again for sharing it with me."

"It really was," she agreed. " If I can be honest, I can't wait to see where this goes, Troy."

Troy's face softened, his smile reaching his eyes. "Neither can I. One step at a time, though, right?"

"Right," she said, feeling a sense of peace settle over her.

As they sat in silence for a moment, she glanced at him with a playful smile. "So, are you always this smooth, or am I just special?"

Troy laughed, the sound deep and genuine. "You're definitely special, Love. I promise I don't go around holding hands with just anyone."

"Good to know," she replied with a teasing glint in her eye.

"You know," he said, his voice quieter now, "I'm really grateful for today. For you."

"Me too," she said, giving his hand a light squeeze.

They sat there for a few moments, not wanting to break the connection. But eventually, they both knew it was time to head inside.

They walked into the lobby together arm in arm, Troy stepped slightly ahead to press the elevator button. The soft ding announced its arrival, and they stepped inside.

The ride up to their floor was quiet, the hum of the elevator the only sound. When they reached her floor, Troy stepped out with Love beside him.

They walked hand in hand to her door.

When they reached her door, she turned to face him.

"Thank you for everything today, Troy. For making me laugh, for listening, for being... being you."

Troy leaned slightly against the doorframe, his hands in his pockets. "And thank you for being you, Love. I've never met anyone like you. I feel like God's up to something special here."

Love smiled; her heart warm. "I feel the same way."

For a moment, neither of them moved. The air between them felt heavy with unspoken emotions, but neither wanted to rush what was clearly unfolding in God's timing.

Troy broke the silence. "Get some rest. We've got a lot of driving ahead of us tomorrow. But if you need anything, you know where to find me."

Love chuckled. "I do Troy, and I will text you if I need anything. Goodnight."

"Goodnight, Love," he said, his tone lingering on her name as though it held more meaning than she realized.

As she stepped into her room and closed the door behind her, Love leaned against it, exhaling deeply. The day had been more than she could have hoped for. God had not only answered her prayers for companionship but had also exceeded her expectations.

She whispered a prayer of gratitude, her heart full. "Thank You, Lord, for today, for Troy, and for the way you're guiding us both. Help us to walk this journey with wisdom and in Your will."

Meanwhile, Troy walked back to his own room right down the hall, replaying the day in his mind. The way Love's smile lit up when she talked about her favorite Bible stories. The peaceful strength she carried when dealing with challenges. The way her faith radiated in everything she did.

As he got back to his room still in thought, he smiled. He got himself showered and prepared to leave the next day. As he lay in bed that night, Troy closed his eyes and prayed. "God, thank you for Love—for her heart, her faith, and the way you've brought her into my life. If this is your will, guide me to honor and cherish her the way you would want me to as your daughter"

******

And with that, they both drifted to sleep, hearts full, dreams laced with hope for what was to come.

CHAPTER 5

The next morning, Sunday, the soft rays of the sun peeked through the curtains, signaling the start of a new day. Love stirred first; she woke up later than normal time but not upset about the additional peaceful sleep she received. She stretched lazily, a peaceful smile gracing her lips as she recalled the warmth of the previous day.

After a quick moment of reflection, she reached for her Bible and journal on the nightstand. Settling back against the pillows, she began her morning devotion, thanking God for the experiences she and Troy had shared and seeking His guidance for what lay ahead today.

Meanwhile, Troy had also woken up later than his normal time, his routine starting with a playlist of worship songs. As the music played softly in the background, he spent a few moments in prayer, expressing his gratitude for Love and asking God to help him lead with intention and honor in today's adventure.

After finishing her prayer, she showered and got dressed. She was packing up her things when her phone buzzed. It was a text from Troy:

"Good morning, Love! How are you feeling? I'm feeling so blessed to start another day with you. When you are ready, can you meet me downstairs at the hotel cafe for breakfast? Thought it'd be nice to grab a quick bite before we hit the road."

Love smiled, typing back quickly:

"Good morning, Troy! I'm feeling blessed also, glad to hear you are. That sounds perfect. Give me 5 minutes.

He stood by the elevator waiting for Love. When he heard the ding of the elevator his heart skipped a beat when he saw Love walking off the elevator. She wore a light blue sundress, simple yet radiant, and her locs framed her face perfectly. Troy exhaled, oh my, he whispered quietly to himself. She was glowing.

"Wow, you look amazing", Troy greeted Love with a warm smile.

She chuckled, "Thank you."

They walked up to the hostess table, she smiled and greeted them, how many? "Two" they responded at the same time, both smiling. She seated them in a booth next to the window where the warm sun shined down on them. They sat their overnight bags on the seat next to them.

How was your morning my love? She blushed, it was great, thanks for asking. I got up a little later than normal but still prayed, did my devotion reading Proverbs 3, meditated on God's word and then some journaling and got myself prepared for our road trip back. Love spoke; her voice thoughtful. "You know the part about trusting in the Lord with all your heart? It reassures me that I don't have to have all the answers. I just need to follow His lead."

Troy nodded, his expression sincere. "I love that. I was praying about the same thing, about letting God lead us and not rushing ahead of His plans. Yesterday felt like such a gift, and I want to make sure we honor Him in whatever comes next on this journey and also our adventures today."

They ordered, she opted for a chai latte and a croissant, while Troy went with black coffee and a blueberry muffin. As they waited, the conversation flowed effortlessly. Love shared how much she'd been looking forward to exploring the museum, especially the ancient manuscripts exhibit and how excited she was to have shared this experience with someone who enjoyed it as much as she did.

"I love how they show the history behind the Scriptures," she said, her eyes lighting up. "It's such a reminder of God's faithfulness through generations."

Troy nodded, leaning forward slightly. "Exactly. It amazes me how God's Word has endured everything: wars, persecution, time itself. It's like holding a piece of eternity in your hands."

Their conversation flowed naturally, moving from scripture to lighthearted topics like their favorite breakfast foods and travel memories.

By the time they finished their breakfast, the nervous energy Troy had felt earlier was gone, replaced with an easy calm.

So Love, would you like to do some sightseeing before we leave or get right on the road, Troy asked inquisitively?

If we have time I would love to ride through the city, get some pictures and maybe some memorabilia to remember our trip.

Troy grinned. "Sounds perfect. I'm up for anything as long as it's with you."

Love laughed, her cheeks flushing slightly. "You're so sweet, you know that?"

"Just being me," Troy said with a wink and stood and offered his hand to help her up.

They exit the booth and Troy grabs both bags and heads to the truck. And with that, they headed out, ready to see what adventures they would go on today. Both of them felt a quiet assurance in their hearts as they walked to the truck that this wasn't just another day it was another step in a journey God was crafting just for them. After settling in the truck, they looked at each other and smiled. "Love your ready"? Troy asked.

"Let's do it," she said, slipping her hand into his.

Well let's get this road trip started, Troy responded."

The drive around the city was filled with laughter and worship music. Troy let Love control the playlist, and she surprised him by picking a song he hadn't heard in a while *"Oceans" by Hillsong United.*

"This was my anthem during a really tough season," Love shared, looking out the window as the music played.

"Really? Same here," Troy said, glancing at her with a smile. "God really meets us in those deep waters, doesn't He?" Troy felt a sense of awe between him and Love and felt the beginnings of a great relationship blossoming. He just looked at her and smiled.

They finally stopped parking near the boardwalk and visited the row of shops on the strip.

They meandered through the streets, popping into boutiques and souvenir shops. Troy noticed Love admiring a delicate bracelet with a cross charm at one store. While she looked at scarfs Troy secretly purchased the bracelet. He wondered if it was too soon to buy gifts. He shook the doubt out of his head knowing that this woman was meant for him and remembering the answer God confirmed the first day he met Love. Walking into another shop that sold Christian memorabilia they looked around. Love picked up a few things to purchase, she showed him a necklace that she was about to purchase. At that moment he was excited to give her the bracelet once she bought the necklace that matched.

They stopped by a few more shops and headed back across the boardwalk to Troy's truck. She stopped to look at the water once more. This place has been so amazing in so many ways and I have enjoyed it so much. Thank you, Lord, she quietly prayed. Troy walked up beside her, Love , thank you for being here with me, being on this trip with you has made me so happy. I wanted to give you something that I saw that reminded me of you.

"This is for you," he said, handing her a small bag as they stood on the pier.

"Oh my goodness Troy!" she exclaimed, her eyes lit up as she opened the bag and saw the bracelet. "You didn't have to do this."

"I wanted to," he replied simply. "It will be beautiful on you." She handed the bracelet back to him and held her wrist out, can you put it on me please, she asked?

Troy fastened the bracelet around her wrist, her heart full. Would you like to put on the matching necklace you bought? She took it out the bag and looked at it, stunned that it did match the bracelet, charm and all even though it was purchased from two different stores. She turned around and let Troy put the necklace on her. He turned back to face him, she looked up at him and smiled. He smiled looking in her eyes, absolutely beautiful. They are, aren't they? "Yes, but I was talking about you, he said". She blushed looking in his eyes, "thank you so much. You have been nothing shy of amazing since I have met you. God must have made you just for me".

He chuckled, "I would have to agree, I have never experienced such peace and surety with someone in my entire life. It seems we are made for each other". They enjoyed the silence for a few more moments then continued back to the truck.

Their exploration continued as they visited a historic church that had been converted into a museum. They marveled at the intricate stained-glass windows and read about the building's rich history.

"Imagine all the prayers that have been lifted up here," Love said softly, her voice tinged with awe.

Troy nodded. "It's humbling. Places like this remind me of how connected we are to generations of faith before us."

As the day stretched on, they found themselves at a bustling outdoor market. The vibrant energy was infectious, with street performers, vendors selling handmade goods, and the tantalizing aroma of food trucks wafting through the air.

"Are you hungry again?" Troy asked with a grin.

"Always," Love laughed, her eyes landing on a vendor selling vegan food.

"Would you be willing to try them," she pointed at the vegan vendor.

"Sure, I will try anything once," Troy laughed.

They made their way over and looked at the menu. They decided to share a plate of vegan wings made out of cauliflower and a slice of vegan pizza, laughing as Troy teased her for having a piece of cheese hanging from her chin.

"That was actually good", Troy said. "Yes, it actually was", Love replied.

As they left the market they stopped by one more spot and grabbed some curly fries.

By the time they made their way back to his truck, the afternoon sun was high in the sky, shining on them. Their hearts are full of the simple joy of spending time together.

"I don't think we could've asked for a better first half of the day," Love said as Troy opened her truck door.

"Agreed," he replied. "But the best part wasn't the sights or the food. It was just being here with you."

Love smiled as she slid into her seat, her heart echoing his sentiment.

CHAPTER 6

As they pulled onto the highway, heading back home, the city they'd explored faded into the distance. But the memories they'd made, and the connection they were building, would stay with them, growing stronger with each mile.

The hum of the tires on the pavement filled the comfortable silence between them, both lost in their own reflections.

Love glanced out the window, a small smile playing on her lips as she thought about the day. She could still feel the warmth of Troy's thoughtful gesture when he gave her the bracelet, the laughter they'd shared over fries, and the quiet reverence of standing in that historic church together.

Troy, with one hand resting on the steering wheel and the other casually draped over the console, stole a glance at her. The way her face lit up when she smiled made his chest tighten, and he couldn't help but thank God for the unexpected gift of her presence in his life.

"You're awfully quiet over there," he said, breaking the silence.

She turned to him, her smile widening. "Just thinking about today. It was perfect."

He chuckled softly. "Perfect, huh? Even with me stealing the best fries?"

"Especially that part," she teased. "It's the little things that make it memorable."

Troy shook his head, laughing. "Well, I'm glad you enjoyed it. I did too. It felt... right, you know? Like this is where we're supposed to be."

Her gaze softened, and she nodded. "Exactly. I've been praying for clarity, and with every moment we've spent together, I feel more at peace."

Troy's grip on the steering wheel tightened slightly as he glanced her way. "Same here. I prayed this morning for God to guide us, and I can honestly say I feel Him in this."

They both fell silent again, the weight of their shared words settling between them like a comforting blanket.

"By the way," Troy said after a moment, "I've been thinking.... I would love to see you often when we return back home. Is that possible?"

Oh yeah? Love asked, his tone playful but curious.

Honestly, Love hesitated. Troy held his breath, waiting on her to finish her stated. I would love to continue to see you. I can't lose the man that God created just for me. Troy let out a sigh of relief.

As the highway stretched ahead of them, they continued to talk about their future plans, dreams, and shared faith. The miles rolled by, but the bond between them only deepened, rooted in the foundation of their love for God and the joy of discovering each other.

As they drove further her mind drifted to something deeper, something she knew she needed to address sooner rather than later.

She had always believed in the clear distinction between dating and courting. Dating, in her view, often lacked direction, a series of encounters without a definitive goal. Courting, however, was purposeful, with marriage as the goal in mind. It wasn't about casually exploring emotions but about building a relationship grounded in faith, mutual respect, and shared values. For her, anything less wasn't an option.

Love glanced out the window at the passing fields, her heart a mix of peace and determination. She knew her journey as a daughter of God had led her to a place where celibacy was non-negotiable. But in today's world, where abstinence was no longer the societal norm, she couldn't help but wonder if Troy understood where she stood—or if he shared the same values.

"Does he already assume this about me because of how vocal I am about my faith? Or do I need to say it out loud?" she thought, her fingers absently tracing the cross on her new bracelet.

Troy must have sensed her shift in energy because he glanced at her with a curious smile. "You okay over there?"

Startled, Love looked at him and returned the smile. "Yeah, just thinking."

"About anything in particular?" he asked, his tone warm and inviting.

She hesitated for a moment, then decided to be honest. "Actually, yes. I've been thinking about something important to me, something I think we should talk about eventually."

Troy's brows curved slightly, but his expression remained gentle. "I'm listening. What's on your mind?"

Love took a deep breath. *Lord, give me the words.*

"Well," she began, her voice steady, "I believe there's a difference between dating and courting. For me, courting has a clear purpose—marriage. I'm not interested in casual relationships or just having fun without any direction." She paused, meeting his gaze for a moment before continuing. "And part of that for me is celibacy. I've made a commitment and a vow to God to wait until marriage, and I want to be upfront about that."

Troy nodded slowly, listening intently as he drove, getting closer to their home exit. "I respect that, Love. And I appreciate you being so open about it."

"Do you feel the same way?" she asked, her voice softer yet nervous.

He took a moment before answering, his tone thoughtful. "I do. I have also committed to waiting until marriage. It hasn't always been easy, but I believe it's worth it—worth honoring God and the person I'm with."

Love felt a wave of relief wash over her, her heart swelling with gratitude. "I'm glad to hear that," she said. "It's just... it's not something everyone understands these days, and I wanted to make sure we were on the same page."

Troy smiled, his expression sincere. "We are. And I'm glad you brought it up. I want our relationship to be built on honesty and a shared belief in what is right. If we're not clear about where we stand, how can we grow together? We have to have a firm foundation in God and in each other."

Her smile widened, and for the first time, she allowed herself to fully relax. This conversation, while daunting, had only confirmed what she was already beginning to see in him—a man of integrity, faith, and purpose.

As they continued down the highway, the atmosphere in the car felt lighter, yet deeper at the same time. They had crossed an important bridge, one that would undoubtedly shape the course of their budding relationship. And for Love, it felt like another confirmation from God that she was walking in His will.

"Love?" Troy said. One thing I want you to promise me. "Yes?" She responded. "Always talk to me if you need clarity on anything. We are both adults and there will be times that you may need charity and confirmation and reassurance. I am okay with giving you what you need when you need. I truly believe that trust can be enhanced by a person's actions, honesty and openness to the needs of their partner".

Love turned to Troy, her heart warming at his sincerity. His tone was steady, but his words carried a depth that she wasn't expecting.

"Troy," she began softly, "I appreciate that more than you know. Communication is everything to me, especially in a relationship. The fact that you're already thinking about how to sustain the trust we have between us means a lot.

He nodded, keeping his eyes on the road but occasionally glancing at her. "I mean it, Love. I want us to be a team, and teams communicate. If you ever feel unsure, or if there's something weighing on you, I want to be the first person you come to. No matter how small or big it is, I'd rather you share it with me than keep it to yourself. I want to be your person."

Love smiled, the sincerity in his voice resonating deeply. "That's rare, Troy. Not everyone thinks like that or is willing to give that kind of reassurance."

He chuckled, his grip on the wheel relaxing slightly. "Well, I've learned that clarity can save a lot of unnecessary misunderstandings. I'd rather talk things through than let assumptions or doubts creep in. Relationships thrive on honesty, and I want ours to thrive."

Her chest tightened in the best way, his words affirming everything she'd been praying for in a partner. She reached over and placed her hand on his. "Yes Troy, I promise. If I need clarity or reassurance, I'll come to you. And I would like you to do the same with me please."

He glanced down at their hands and smiled. "Deal."

Love leaned back in her seat, the comfort of their understanding settling over her like a warm blanket. "You know," she said, a playful lift in her voice, "you're making it really hard not to like you more and more."

Troy laughed, his deep, rich chuckle filling the car. "Good. Because I plan to keep doing that."

As the highway stretched ahead of them, Love couldn't help but feel an overwhelming sense of peace. Troy's commitment to openness and trust mirrored her own values, and it reinforced what she already suspected, that this was the kind of relationship she'd been praying for. A relationship rooted in their faith, truth, and intentionality.

As the miles slipped away and the familiar scenery of home began to come into view, Troy glanced over at Love, who was gazing out the window, a serene smile on her face. He could feel the anticipation building in his chest—it had been an incredible weekend, and he wasn't ready to let their connection pause until their next meeting.

"So, Love," he said, his voice warm and steady, "can we talk about the next time I get to see you?"

She turned toward him, her smile widening. "Already planning our next adventure, huh?"

He chuckled, keeping his eyes on the road. "Absolutely. After spending this time with you, I don't want to wait too long to do it again. I've been spoiled now."

Love laughed softly, the sound filling the car with warmth. "Spoiled, huh? Well, I guess I can't blame you—this weekend has been amazing."

"It really has," Troy agreed. "So, what do you think? Do we make good on the Ark Encounter idea? Or do you have something else in mind?"

She tilted her head thoughtfully. "The Ark Encounter is definitely on my list, but maybe for something a little sooner, we could keep it simple. Maybe dinner and a gospel concert or even a day at a botanical garden? What do you think?"

Troy nodded, a smile playing on his lips. "I love both ideas. Dinner and live music would give us a chance to relax and enjoy some uplifting music, and the garden would be great for conversation—and maybe more of your famous random Bible trivia."

She laughed. "Don't act like you didn't enjoy every second of my trivia questions."

"Okay, you got me," he admitted, laughing aloud. "I'll happily lose to you in Bible trivia anytime."

Love's expression softened, her playful demeanor giving way to a more serious tone. "Thank you, Troy. For this weekend, for being intentional, and for wanting to plan more time together. It means a lot to me."

Troy glanced at her briefly, his eyes warm. "It's not hard to be intentional with someone like you, Love. You make it easy to want to invest time and effort."

Her heart swelled at his words, and she felt a quiet gratitude for the way he saw her.

"Okay," she said, smiling again, "let's plan for dinner and live music first.

"Perfect," he said without hesitation.

As the car continued down the highway, the thought of their next moments together filled the air with excitement and promise. They were both certain of one thing, this was only the beginning of something special.

The final stretch of the drive was filled with comfortable conversation and laughter as they fleshed out the details of their next meeting.

"So," Troy said, glancing at her with a playful grin, "dinner and a concert it is. Any particular type of music you'd like? Or are we sticking to the gospel all the way?"

Love raised an eyebrow, smirking. "Well, since you're so enthusiastic about planning, how about I leave that up to you? Surprise me."

"Careful now," Troy teased. "I might show up with tickets to something completely unexpected."

Love laughed. "I trust you. Just make sure it's something uplifting—or at least something we can sing to."

"Challenge accepted," Troy said, tapping the steering wheel.

As the conversation drifted to lighter topics, Love found herself reflecting on how easy it was to talk to him. Whether they were planning future dates or joking about trivial things, Troy had a way of making her feel at ease—like she could be fully herself without any pretense.

The sign for their exit came into view, and Troy turned on his blinker. "Almost home," he said, his tone was a mix of contentment and a hint of reluctance. "I wish this weekend didn't have to end so soon."

Love nodded. "I feel the same way. But it's not really the end, it's just the beginning, right?"

He looked at her briefly, his expression soft. "Right."

******

As they pulled into her driveway, Troy parked the car and turned off the engine. He turned to her, his gaze warm and full of intention.

"Thank you for this weekend, Love," he said. "For your time, your conversation, and just... being you."

Love smiled, her heart full. "Thank you, Troy. For being thoughtful, for making me feel safe, special, and for being such a gentleman. This weekend was perfect."

He stepped out of the car and quickly came around to her side, opening the door for her. "Chivalry, remember?" he said with a wink.

She laughed as she grabbed his extended hand and stepped out. "It's noted and very much appreciated."

They walked together to her door, the evening air cool and quiet around them. Troy turned to her, pausing as if gathering his thoughts.

"I'll call you tomorrow," he said. "But before I go, can I pray with you one more time?"

Love's eyes lit up, and she nodded. "I'd love that."

Standing on her porch, their hands joined, Troy offered a prayer of gratitude for the time they'd spent together, for safe travels, and for the journey ahead—both individually and together.

When he finished, Love squeezed his hand gently. "Thank you, Troy. For everything."

He smiled, his eyes holding hers for a moment before he stepped back toward his car. "Goodnight, Love. I'll talk to you soon."

"Goodnight, Troy, please text me when you get home so I know you made it safe" she said. He nodded and walked back to his truck. She went inside but stood at the door watching as he drove off into the night.

As she closed the door behind her, Love leaned against it, her heart full of gratitude and excitement for the experiences they had shared and the ones to come. For the first time in a long time, she felt like her prayers were truly unfolding right before her eyes. Love sighed softly as she locked the door and set her purse on the entryway table. Her home was quiet, but her heart was alive with the echoes of the weekend. She replayed the moments—the museum, the walk on the boardwalk, their nighty conversations. Every detail seemed to whisper that something special was blooming.

She made her way to her bedroom and sat on the edge of her bed, pulling her journal out of her overnight bag. Love had made it a habit to write down her prayers, thoughts, and reflections—a practice that kept her grounded in her walk with God.

She flipped to a fresh page and began to write:

Lord, thank You for this weekend. Thank You for the time I got to spend with Troy and for the way he honors You in his words and actions. Thank You for showing me what it looks like to connect with someone who shares the same values and love for You. I don't know where this is going, but I trust you to lead us both according to your will. Please continue to guide us and give me wisdom to navigate this new season.

After she finished writing, Love leaned back against her pillows, her mind wandering to the last conversation she'd had with Troy. His willingness to pray with her, to listen, to be intentional all aligned with the qualities she had prayed for in a future husband.

But even as her heart fluttered with excitement, Love knew she needed to remain prayerful and discerning. She didn't want to get caught up in emotions without seeking God's direction every step of the way. Love showered and got in her bed and fell asleep effortlessly.

CHAPTER 7

Monday morning came quickly, Love woke with her thoughts still lingering on the weekend. She didn't realize that she overslept so she didn't have much time for prayer, devotion, and journaling. She was so high off the weekend she obviously slept through the alarm. She spent 30 minutes in prayer and another 30 minutes reading her devotion, doing meditation and journaling before getting ready for work. She decided to call her best friend, Jasmine, while on the way to work to share her experience and get some perspective.

"Hey, girl," Jasmine said as she answered the call. "You're calling me early, what's going on?"

"Morning!" Love replied, a smile evident in her voice. "I wanted to tell you about my weekend. It was... amazing."

Jasmine gasped dramatically. "Amazing? Spill it, Love. Don't leave me hanging!"

Love laughed, recounting the trip to the Bible Museum, the walk on the boardwalk, and Troy's thoughtful gestures. Jasmine listened intently, occasionally chiming in with affirmations and playful teasing.

"Girl," Jasmine said when Love finished, "it sounds like he's a good one. And the fact that he's praying with you? That's rare these days."

"I know," Love agreed. "It feels different, Jas. But I'm being cautious. I want to make sure I'm listening to God through all of this."

"That's wise," Jasmine said. "Just take it one day at a time. But from what you're telling me, he sounds intentional—and that's a great foundation."

As the conversation ended, Love felt even more confident about the weekend and the connection she was building with Troy.

Later that day, her phone buzzed with a message from him:

Good afternoon, Love. Just wanted to say I'm thinking of you and looking forward to seeing you again real soon. Hope your day is going as amazing as you are.

She couldn't help but smile as she typed a reply:

Thank you, Troy. My day's been great. I'm looking forward to seeing you soon also. How is your day going so far?

As she hit the send button, Love couldn't shake the feeling that this was only the beginning of something to last a lifetime and enjoying every moment.

Her phone buzzed again almost immediately.

Troy's reply came through:

My day has been good, but you just made it better. Can I call you later? I'd love to hear your voice.

Love's heart flipped a little as she read his words. She appreciated his consistency and his effort to communicate. It was refreshing, and it warmed her spirit.

I'd like that, she replied simply, not wanting to come across as too eager, even though she was already looking forward to it.

The rest of her day seemed to fly by. Between work and errands, Love was busy but couldn't help but think about the connection she and Troy were forming. She thanked God for the clarity she felt and the peace that surrounded this blossoming relationship.

That evening, right on time, her phone rang. Seeing Troy's name on the screen, she smiled as she answered.

"Hello, Troy," she said, her tone soft but cheerful.

"Hello, Love," he replied, his voice warm and steady. "How's my favorite lady doing?"

She chuckled lightly. "I'm doing well. And you?"

"Even better now," he said, the sincerity in his voice unmistakable.

Their conversation flowed effortlessly, just as it had over the weekend. They talked about their day, shared funny stories about work, and even discussed a sermon Troy had listened to earlier.

"Have you ever thought about how important it is to protect your peace?" Troy asked, his tone thoughtful.

"Absolutely," Love replied. "It's something I've been learning a lot about lately. God's peace is such a gift, but it's up to us to guard it, you know?"

"Exactly," Troy said. "I think that's one of the things I admire about you—you seem to carry that peace with you. It's inspiring."

Love felt her cheeks warm at his words. "Thank you, Troy. That means a lot coming from you. I haven't always been like this, it has taken a lot of prayer."

As their conversation deepened, they began talking about their goals and dreams, their favorite devotion, and how they each came to know Christ. By the time they said goodnight, Love felt even more confident that this connection was God-orchestrated.

"Goodnight, Love," Troy said, his voice gentle. "Sleep well, and I'll talk to you soon."

"Goodnight, Troy," she replied, her voice soft with contentment.

As she laid her phone down, Love closed her eyes and whispered a prayer of gratitude for the future and plan that God has for her and Troy and for them both to have a very peaceful sleep. She felt good covering him in prayer knowing that God has already told her that Troy is her future.

Before she knew it three months had flown by, and it was already the last Wednesday in October. She and Troy had been talking every day and they both were enjoying every minute of getting to know each other in this budding romance they both knew was there. Love looked at her watch and realized it was almost time for lunch, and she had to get ready to go to meet Troy for lunch. When they began spending time together, they agreed that they can meet 2-3 times a week at their "spot" Jazzy's Lounge for lunch.

In the next moment Julie, Love's admin assistant, stepped into the doorway of her office. "Yes ma'am?" Love noticed her assistant at her door as she searched her drawer for her keys.

"Ms. Wilson, are you going out for lunch today?" Julie asked.

"Yes ma'am, I am meeting someone during my lunch hour", she said with a slight smile. She looked up to see Julie with tears in her eyes. Oh goodness what's wrong, Love stood and called Julie over to her. Julie came closer, my mom just called, and they rushed my dad to the ER. They think he had a heart attack" she said, her voice full of sadness.

"Oh no, go Julie, everything here will be fine. Go! Don't worry about coming back today and please call me to let me know about your dad. I will be praying for him, you and your mom. I know you are upset but be safe driving there" Love said with concern. "Yes ma'am" Julie said as she turned and hurried to get her things and leave. Love sat back at her desk, clasped her hands together and closed her eyes. As she began to pray, she heard a voice at her door, "Is everything okay Love?"

She looked up from her prayer and saw Mr. Harold, her boss, standing there. "I just saw Julie almost running out of here, is everything okay?" "No sir, her dad was rushed to the ER with signs of a heart attack. I told her to go ahead and leave for the day. I know we are waiting for an answer from Johnson and Everett Firm so I will stay to make sure I don't miss it."

"Oh no I hope her dad is okay, I remember when I had my heart attack, it is nothing to play with. Thank you for being so involved but you can take your lunch this is why we have voicemail, he advised."

"It's okay Mr. Harold. I know we may need to negotiate so I don't want to miss this call".

"Thank you for being so diligent with this project," he said.

Always sir, I take my job very seriously and I love what I do, Love responded.

Okay well let me know if there is anything I can do, he said with sincerity.

Yes sir, she responded, thank you sir, Love responded with a smile.

She took her phone out of her purse and realized that she had missed 2 calls from Troy and a text asking if she was okay. She returned his call.

"Hey, my Love, is everything okay?" he said quickly. Yes, my assistant Julie, Love started. Her dad was rushed to the ER with the possibility of a heart attack, and I told her to leave to go be with her family. So, I'm going to be at the office through lunch waiting on the phone call from a client about the project that I am heading up.

My goodness, Troy said with concern in his voice. I pray her dad is okay and I know that you have to stay at the office. I am just glad you are okay because when you didn't show and I couldn't get you on the phone I began to get worried.

"I'm okay but when she rushed out my boss was concerned, and he was standing in my office for a moment talking to me. I know this is disappointing and I will make it up to you", Love stated.

"Make it up to me huh", he said inquisitively. "Yes, for being so understanding and patient with this last-minute change to our plans", she responded.

"I understand that there are times when things can change abruptly and I know you will always communicate with me", he said with deep confidence in his voice.

"Yes I will absolutely always communicate because you're my person", she replied.

"Your person?", he questioned with a smile? "Yes, Troy you are now my person". She giggled; he chuckled. They sat in sweet silence for just a moment when her other line beeped in. "Oh Troy this is the client, I have to take this, I'll call you back as soon as I am done."

"Okay I'll be waiting", he said quickly.

"Okay, love you, bye", she quickly responded. As she clicked over, she was stunned at the words that left her lips in Troy's ears. Hopefully he didn't hear me, she thought.

"Hello", the male voice from the other end of the phone spoke up, confused by the silence.

"Oh, yes I am here, I apologize. This is Love Wilson; how may I help you?"

"Hello Ms. Wilson, this is Jeff Everett with Johnson and Everett, how are you?"

"I'm good, thank you for reaching out today." Love responded.

"Of course, I wanted to make contact prior to my trip for the holidays because I will be leaving today and not returning until after the New Year."

She puts him on speakerphone and gets up to shut her office door. "Sounds awesome, I hope you have an amazing time on vacation." she said.

"Yes, I plan to," he chuckled. "Well Ms. Wilson I hate to rush this conversation; however, I have to get to the airport within the next hour. So, I am calling to tell you that the firm has agreed to your terms for the project. No need for negotiation, we will give you whatever you need to get everything completed. Can you advise when the project is set to begin", he asked.

"The contractors have agreed to begin construction at the beginning of January," Love replied.

"That's awesome we thought it would be by March, so does that mean we may have everything completed earlier than expected", he asked.

"Yes, that is the plan that has been set up", she smiled.

"Ms. Wilson, that is great news and I am happy to hear that so I can really enjoy my travels and vacation now. Thank you for all you all do for us. Have the most amazing holiday season. Should you need me please email me but if not we will speak again after New Year," Jeff states.

"You too, Mr. Everett, we will speak next year, be blessed sir," she said cheerfully.

As they hung up the call there was a knock at her door.

"Come in," she says. The door opens and Mark the receptionist sticks his head in and states that she has a visitor. I wonder who that can be, she thought since she had no appointments scheduled.

"Send them in please, thanks Mark."

She pulled up her calendar and quickly updated her meeting events and sent a message to Mr. Harold about the great news from Jeff Everett. He had left the office for the day so she knew he would see this in the morning.

Her door opens again and in steps Troy with a dozen vibrant blue and white calla lilies and a bag from their favorite lunch spot. She was smiling at the sight of Troy standing in her doorway. She stood, "Heyyyy handsome please come in and you can shut the door" she stated.

She couldn't help but blush at the sight of this beautiful man she was in love with coming into her office. "Troyyyyy, what are you doing here?" she asked, completely surprised.

Well, I knew you hadn't eaten and I know you are also worried about Julie so I wanted to surprise you and bring you food. She walked around her desk and hugged him tight. He slightly hugged her back because his hands were full. He whispered, "Can I put these down please?" Oh yes, Love responded. She stepped back to let him get to her desk. He put the flowers and the food down. She sat in a chair in front of her desk, after putting the items on her desk he turned and saw her sitting, he reached for her, pulled her back up and into his arms giving her a very comforting embrace. She almost melted into his arms not even realizing that she needed that hug. He slowly released her and they both sat.

She looked down nervously recalling what she said prior to switching the call over to Jeff. "What's wrong, beautiful? Did you get news on Julie's father," he asked with concern?

She slowly looked up at him and nervously said, "ummm no not that but about what I said earlier". He put his hand up to stop her. He grabbed her hand "Love, it's okay no need to explain". She said, "no I um". She closed her eyes. "Troy I"....

"Love listen", Troy cut her off, "I know you like me so there is no need to apologize for saying it before you felt it, I'm sure you said it because of the call coming in and what happened with Julie and so much happening all at one time".

"Wait, apologize?" She asked with a raised eyebrow. "Why would I apologize", she asked?

"I thought maybe you said it but didn't mean it", he responded.

She moved her chair closer and looked at him eye to eye. "Troy, let me be honest, I meant what I said, I do love you", she paused, "I know it's out of the blue, but I did mean it. I just was not expecting it to come out so suddenly and during a phone call. Plus I wanted to wait until you were ready and said it first".

"Why did you want me to say it first?", he chuckled.

"Well because you are the man. I don't want to seem too eager or like I am moving too fast", she replied.

He smiled, "you cannot move too fast. I am completely ready for what is growing between us. I love this, I love us, and Love, I love you also," he said confidently."

She looked at him with tears in her eyes, "you mean that" she asked? "Yes, with everything in me. I wanted to tell you that I loved you the same night as the museum visit, but I did not want to scare you off."

"Are you serious," she blushed. "Yes, I have never felt like this and I know what I want," he said.

"Which is what," she asked. "YOU, Love, I know I want you", he said with determination. "I couldn't have asked for a better blessing from God". "Can I be honest", he asked? "Yes," she replied. "I hope you don't think I am crazy, but I know you are my wife, God told me the day I met you. Because I know you are my wife I want to properly court you, I want to be exclusive."

Love stood up and walked to her window and closed her eyes. Troy got up and walked up beside her, he put his hands on her shoulders. Love, look at me, please, he requested. She turned and looked at him with tears in her eyes. "Why are you sad?" Troy asked. "Am I moving too fast?"

"No" Troy she quickly responded, "I am happy. This is what I have prayed for", she replied. "A man that loves God more than himself, a man that will pray with me, for and over me, and man that wants to pursue and court me for real. A man that will go to God before making a move and asking God to be with me, with us. This is my prayer and has been my prayer for most of my life and I am so excited. The tears are happy tears not sad tears" she said intently.

"Love, you are the woman I prayed for, he started. "You are the Wife I prayed for. When God confirmed and told me it was you I was speechless because I prayed for my Wife to be filled with his spirit and to have evidence of the fruits of his spirit, love God with all that she has, not ashamed of her love for God, willing to stay pure no matter the temptations of the flesh, to be willing to submit along with me to God and to each other, to have fun together, travel, enjoy life as one. And everything I prayed for and more you possess as the woman of God that you are. God gives us our needs and sometimes our wants. God gave me all that and added stunning beauty to my Wife. How can I not thank him?"

"Troy," Love started, her tone becoming more reflective, "I've been thinking a lot about what it means to be intentional in relationships. You know, not just going through the motions but really building something that honors God."

He nodded, his expression serious yet soft. "I feel the same way. I've wasted time in the past, just dating for the sake of dating. But now? I want something real. A partnership that's grounded in faith and purpose. And I'm learning that it takes time, effort, and a lot of prayer."

"Exactly," she agreed, her voice laced with passion. "It's about more than feelings, it's about commitment and vision. That's why courting feels so different to me. It's not just about seeing where things go; it's about heading in a direction with clarity."

Troy leaned forward, resting his elbows on the table. "Love, I respect that so much about you. From the moment we met, I could see that you're a woman who knows what she wants and isn't afraid to stand firm in her faith. That's rare, and it's something I admire deeply."

Her heart warmed at his words, and for a moment, she was at a loss for what to say.

"Troy," she finally said, her voice soft but steady, "thank you. That means a lot to me. And for what it's worth, I see that same strength in you. Your intentionality, your kindness—it's refreshing."

They held each other's gaze for a moment, the silence between them filled with unspoken understanding as if they could see each other's souls.

Does this conversation mean you will be my woman, exclusively, can I court you properly, he asked?

CHAPTER 8

With the biggest smile she softly answered "yes, I haven't wanted anyone else since we met. I was celibate even before I met you, I refused to settle, I only wanted the Husband God has for me and here you are".

He kissed her forehead and hugged her and held her close. She stayed in his embrace for a few moments. He released her, smiled, kissed her forehead once more then went to sit back in front of her desk. Do you mind if I sit with you while you eat your lunch? "Sure", she smiled. She sat at her desk unpacked her lunch and prepared to eat.

Her phone buzzed, it was Jasmine asking about the Friday night service at her church and if Love would be able to make it. She looked up at Troy. "Troy, would you like to go to church with me Friday night? It's at my best friend's church."

"Oh now I'm sure I am yours, I get to meet your best friend", he chuckled. "Yes, I would love to go on a church date with you". "Awesome," Love responded.

She texted Jasmine that she would be there with a plus one and that she would call her later. Jasmine sent back the heart emojis.

As Love opened the container, the aroma of her favorite meal filled the room. She paused and looked at Troy, her eyes wide with surprise.

"Troy, you got my favorite lunch?" she asked, her tone filled with warmth and curiosity.

He leaned back in his chair, a small smile playing on his lips. "Of course. I pay a great deal of attention to you, Love. Your movements, your body language, what you like and don't like, your facial expressions—everything."

Her smile deepened as she felt a blush creeping up her cheeks. She took a moment to absorb his words, her heart swelling with gratitude.

"Thank you, Troy," she said softly, her voice laced with sincerity. "That means more to me than you know."

He nodded, his gaze steady but kind. "You deserve someone who sees you, Love. Not just the surface, but who you really are. And I'm here to do just that."

She sighed, a grateful, contented sigh, and picked up a wing. "Well, these wings and okra are a great start," she teased with a playful grin.

They both laughed, the atmosphere light and easy. As Love enjoyed her meal, they continued talking about their plans for the weekend.

"I was thinking," Troy said, leaning forward slightly, "since the weather is supposed to be cool but nice, we can go to the park. Maybe even pack a little picnic? Something simple."

Love nodded, her eyes lighting up. "That sounds perfect. I will love that. It'll be nice to spend time outside and just... enjoy the moment since the weather has not really gotten cold."

Troy smiled, clearly pleased with her response. "Then it's a date," he said confidently.

As Love finished her last bite, she leaned back and sighed with contentment. "That hit the spot. Thank you for this, Troy."

"Anything for you," he said simply, his voice warm.

In that moment, Love realized how much she appreciated Troy's thoughtfulness and attention to detail. It wasn't just the food—it was the way he made her feel seen and valued.

As Love pushed her plate aside and wiped her hands, she glanced at Troy with a playful smile.

"Okay, Mr. Thoughtful, what other surprises do you have up your sleeve?" she teased, tilting her head.

Troy chuckled, leaning back in his chair. "I guess you'll just have to wait and see. Can't give away all my secrets, now can I?"

She laughed, shaking her head. "Fair enough. But you've set the bar pretty high with this lunch. Just so you know."

"Challenge accepted," he said with a wink, making her laugh even more.

"So, we have a lunch date tomorrow, church date Friday and picnic date on Saturday", Troy confirmed. "Can we make an entire weekend of time together as an official couple, can I invite you to church Sunday and then go out to eat after"?

"Yes, to all of these dates, just let me know the time on Saturday and Sunday, and I'll be ready."

"Perfect," he said, his smile widening. "What time do I need to get to you for church Friday"?

"Well, service starts at 7pm so maybe 6-615".

Troy nodded, mentally noting the time. "Got it. I'll be there by 6, no later than 6:15. I want to make sure we have plenty of time to get there without feeling rushed."

Love smiled, appreciating his punctuality and thoughtfulness. "Sounds perfect. I'm looking forward to the rest of this week and weekend together."

Troy leaned back in his chair, his expression warm. "I agree. Spending time with you is always awesome but now I can say you are my woman, my lady, my love, my future wife, my everything, he smiled.

She nodded, yes I am your everything! Her heart was swelling with joy. "This is what I've always wanted, Troy." A relationship where this kind of love isn't just something we talk about but something we actively live out together."

"And that's exactly what I want too, Love. Love is indeed an action word," he said earnestly. "I can already tell these days will be memorable just like the last three months, because of the memories we are making together." "So, about Sunday—my church service starts at 10 a.m. We'll need to leave by 9:15 to get there on time. Afterward, we can grab food at one of my favorite spots.

Her cheeks flushed at his words, "Deal," Love said with a grin. "So, to recap: Church date tomorrow evening, picnic Saturday, and church again Sunday morning with lunch afterward. A whole weekend with you—I couldn't ask for more."

"I'm excited about every single moment we'll get to spend together."

As they finished their conversation, Love felt a deep sense of gratitude. It wasn't just about the plans they were wonderful, yes but it was about the intentionality and effort Troy was putting into their relationship. It is so refreshing, she thought.

"Alright, Mr. Planner," she said playfully as they stood up. "I'll see you tomorrow for lunch."

"You can count on it, and every day thereafter" Troy replied, his voice steady and reassuring.

As Love walked him to the door, she felt a sense of peace settle over her. Today starts a new chapter, one filled with purpose, faith, and the kind of connection she had prayed for. And she can't wait to see how it will unfold.

CHAPTER 9

The next day seemed to fly by, each hour blending seamlessly into the next. Since deciding to court and officially beginning their relationship yesterday, Love and Troy knew they would be spending every possible moment together, cherishing intentional time as they built their connection.

Thursday started off like any other day—calm and uneventful. Troy had called Love to postpone their normal lunch date and advise that something had come up but promised her that she would see him later. Love understood but wondered if everything was okay. She moved through her day quietly with a prayerful heart for Troy who was on her mind especially since she hadn't heard from him since canceling their lunch plans.

Love was just about to leave for the day when her phone rang.

"Hello?" she answered, her tone curious.

"Hello, Ms. Love," a warm, professional voice replied. "This is Daniel. I've been sent to pick you up."

"Pick me up?" Love asked, her brows furrowing.

"Yes, ma'am," Daniel confirmed. "I was hired to drive you to your date with Mr. Hayes."

Love hesitated for a moment, a mix of surprise and intrigue flashing across her face. "Umm... okay. I'll be right down," she said, a slight smile tugging at her lips as her curiosity grew.

When she stepped outside, her eyes were immediately drawn to a sleek black car parked by the curb. A tall gentleman in a tailored suit stood beside it, his demeanor calm and composed.

"Daniel?" she asked as she approached cautiously.

"Yes, Ms. Love," he replied with a polite nod, opening the car door with a practiced gesture.

Love hesitated, her steps slowing as she peeked inside. Her breath caught at the sight before her—a mixture of roses and calla lilies in each of her favorite colors. Blue, purple, red, white, and yellow blooms filled the seat and floor beside her, leaving her just enough room to slide in and place her bag beside her, their fragrance enveloping the space.

"Wow," she murmured, sliding into the car carefully as if she didn't want to disturb the delicate arrangement, placing her bag beside her.

Daniel closed the door gently, and as Love settled in, her eyes fell on a small note nestled within one of the bundles. She plucked it out and unfolded it, her heart skipping a beat as she read:

Hey my Love,

I apologize for canceling lunch today.

I had something greater planned for you, for us!

I am waiting for you to join me for an amazing dinner.

I look forward to seeing you, momentarily.

Thank you for trusting Daniel to bring you here.

And thank you for trusting me to love you

and treat you like the Queen you are.

See you soon, my Love.

-Troy.

A soft smile spread across her face as she folded the note and glanced out the window. Her mind raced with thoughts about what Troy might have planned, each idea more exciting than the last.

The car came to a smooth stop in front of a stunning downtown building. Love's eyes widened as she took in the scene— tall, elegant windows framed with intricate designs, grand Victorian doors, and a vibrant red carpet stretching across the entrance. Love's anticipation bubbled in her chest as she gazed at the building.

Daniel stepped out to open her door once more. "Here we are, Ms. Love," he said, offering her a reassuring smile.

Love stepped out, taking in the grandeur of the building before her once again. She smoothed her skirt nervously, Daniel gestured toward the doors, offering her his arm. "This way, ma'am." Love took his arm hesitantly, her eyes darting around as she tried to piece together what Troy had planned. The tall, arched windows of the building revealed a soft glow of candlelight inside, heightening the mystery.

As the doors opened, Love gasped softly. The interior was breathtaking. The room was bathed in warm, golden light, with a stunning chandelier overhead. A single table was set in the center of the room, adorned with a crisp white tablecloth, elegant silverware, and a centerpiece of calla lilies, her favorite flowers.

And there, standing by the table, was Troy. He wore a sharp navy blazer and a warm smile that made Love's heart skip a beat.

"Hey, my Love," he said, his voice steady and affectionate.

"Troy," she breathed, taking in the sight of him and the effort he'd put into this moment. "What is all of this?"

He walked closer, taking her hands gently in his. "This is just a small way to show you how much I appreciate you and love you. How much

I cherish the time we've been spending together. I wanted to make today a little extra special."

Love smiled, her eyes glistening. "You have absolutely done that."

"I want you to always know that you deserve the best," Troy said simply. He guided her to the table, pulling out her chair before taking his seat across from her.

As they settled, a waiter appeared from behind the curtain, dressed sharply in black and white, walking towards them carrying a tray with two crystal glasses of sparkling cider. They grabbed the glasses.

"To us," Troy said, raising his glass once the waiter poured.

"To us," Love echoed, clinking her glass softly against his.

The first course arrived shortly after—a delicate plate of creamy tomato bisque served with a slice of freshly baked rosemary bread. The aroma of the herbs and the rich soup filled the air as they shared smiles and light conversation.

"This soup is incredible," Love said after her first spoonful.

"I'm glad you like it," Troy replied. "I may have had a hand in picking the menu."

Next came the main course: a perfectly seared salmon fillet topped with a lemon-butter sauce, served alongside garlic mashed potatoes and roasted asparagus. The plates were beautifully arranged, almost too pretty to eat.

Love took a bite of the salmon, her eyes widening. "Troy, this is amazing. Did you plan all of this yourself?"

He nodded, his expression softening. "I wanted everything to be just right for you. You're worth the effort."

Love smiled, her cheeks warming as she savored another bite.

They opened up about how they saw life together, their dreams and aspirations. The connection between them deepened with each moment together.

Finally, dessert arrived—a decadent chocolate lava cake paired with fresh raspberries and a drizzle of caramel. The rich aroma of cocoa filled the air as the waiter set the plates down.

"I think this might be my favorite part," Love said with a laugh, her fork sinking into the warm, gooey center of the cake.

Troy chuckled. "I had a feeling you'd say that."

As the meal concluded, Troy reached across the table and took her hand in his. His touch was warm and steady, grounding her in the moment.

"Love," he said, his voice soft but firm, "I know we're just starting this journey together, but I want you to know how much I care and love you. Every day with you feels like a blessing, and I look forward to what each day brings between us and learning you more and more."

Her eyes glistened as she squeezed his hand. "I feel the same way, Troy. Thank you for today. It's more than I could've ever imagined."

He smiled, his gaze filled with affection. "This is just the beginning, Love. I promise you that."

The waiter discreetly cleared their plates, leaving the table clear except for their glasses and the stunning calla lily centerpiece. Troy stood and extended his hand to Love.

"Come with me," he said, his voice low and inviting.

Love hesitated for a moment, curiosity flickering in her eyes. "Where are we going?"

"You'll see," he replied with a playful grin.

She placed her hand in his, letting him guide her through a side door of the grand dining room. They stepped into a softly lit hallway, the faint sound of piano music drifting through the air. As they walked, Love noticed framed photographs lining the walls, each capturing moments of joy—weddings, family gatherings, and celebrations.

Troy stopped in front of a set of French doors and turned to her. "Close your eyes."

She tilted her head, a teasing smile on her lips. "Troy, more surprises?"

"Trust me," he said gently.

With a soft laugh, she closed her eyes, her hand still clasped in his. She could tell as they continued to walk that they were waking up a ramp then she heard the doors creak open and felt the cool evening air brush against her skin.

"Okay, open them," Troy said.

Love's eyes fluttered open, and she gasped. They stood on a rooftop terrace adorned with twinkling fairy lights. The city skyline stretched out before them, its lights sparkling like diamonds against the night sky. Under the twinkling lights she saw where the piano music was originating. He set up the live music with dinner as they discussed previously. Love was amazed that he remembered. "Troy, is this the date we talked about?" He smiled, "yes my love I remembered." They walked to the middle of the open space, and he extended his hand once more but this time to dance with her. They danced seamlessly through several songs enjoying each other's movements. Troy noticed that the temperature was dropping. "It's getting chilly, let's have a seat before we call it a night my love." Troy turned her once more in a swift dancing movement. On the right side of the terrace was a small fire pit surrounded by a plush loveseat and a few single chairs with a cozy blanket draped over the love seat.

"Troy," she whispered. "I love it"

He guided her to the love seat and wrapped the blanket around her shoulders before sitting down beside her. A tray with two mugs of steaming mocha cappuccino and a plate of freshly baked cookies were placed before them by the same server as before.

"I thought we could end the evening here," he said, handing her a mug.

Love smiled, taking a sip of the rich, creamy mocha. "You've thought of everything, haven't you?"

He chuckled. "I just wanted tonight to be special."

As they sat beneath the stars, the conversation shifted to the 3 F's faith, family, and the future. Troy shared his vision for a Christ-centered life and his dreams of building a home filled with love and laughter.

"I want my life to be a reflection of God's goodness," he said, his voice steady. "And I know that includes the people I choose to surround myself with. Love, being with you has only strengthened my faith. I feel like God brought us together for a reason."

Her heart swelled at his words, and she placed her hand over his. "Troy, you've shown me what it means to be loved with intention. I thank God for you every day."

He smiled, his eyes filled with warmth. "I feel the same way." Troy leaned back in his chair, his gaze thoughtful as he stared out at the twinkling city lights. Then he turned to Love, his expression earnest.

"Once I gave my life to God, I envisioned a life where everything I do, every decision I make, reflects God's purpose for me," he began, his voice steady and filled with conviction. "A Christ-centered life isn't just about going to church on Sundays or saying the right things—it's about how I live, how I forgive, how I love, and how I serve. I want my home to be a sanctuary, a place where faith is the foundation, and love is the atmosphere."

Love listened intently, captivated by the depth of his words.

"I picture a home where God's presence is felt in every room," Troy continued. "Where we start and end each day in prayer, seeking His guidance even in what I wear. A home where laughter fills the walls, even in hard times, because we know our joy comes from Him."

He paused, a small smile touching his lips. "I want a family that grows together spiritually, where we support each other and encourage each other to walk in our purpose and achieve our goals in our natural life and spiritual life. A place where we celebrate God's blessings and lean on Him when things get tough."

Love felt her heart swell as she imagined the life Troy described—a life of unity, purpose, and unwavering faith.

"And I don't just want a house," Troy said, his eyes locking with hers. "I want a home. A place where we can be ourselves, you know how people say they want to "fall" in love, I want to grow in love with you. Grow closer to God together, build a relationship that honors Him—reading scripture together, serving others as a family, and creating memories that reflect His love."

He reached for her hand, his thumb gently brushing over hers. "Love, I believe God calls us to be intentional in everything we do, especially when it comes to building a life with someone. And with you, I see a future filled with purpose, love, and endless possibilities."

Her eyes glistened with unshed tears as she smiled at him, her heart overwhelmed by his sincerity. "Troy, what you're describing isn't just a dream—it's a ministry. A life that reflects God's glory in every way."

He nodded, his smile growing. "Exactly. That's what I want—a life that honors Him, with a partner who shares the same vision. And Love... I see that partner in you."

Her breath hitched at his words, and for a moment, all she could do was hold his gaze. The city lights seemed to dim in comparison to the brightness of their connection, and Love felt an unshakable certainty in her spirit that God was weaving their hearts together for His purpose, the growing love and passion that will carry them further than any natural love.

CHAPTER 10

Friday flew by for Love, her day filled with work, meetings, and the lingering thoughts of the night before. Excitement bubbled within her as she anticipated the church date with Troy that evening. She was walking on a cloud from the night before and the amazing date he set up.

Love wrapped up her workday at 3 PM, relieved to have an early start on her evening preparations. She headed home, where she carefully chose an outfit and began getting ready for Troy's arrival at 6.

Meanwhile, Troy's day was quieter but no less productive. His only scheduled obligation was a noon staff meeting, which he decided to have catered and show appreciation for his staff. He ordered from Jazzy's Lounge, he and Love's favorite spot, ensuring his team would enjoy the meal.

Troy sat in his office, lost in thought about Love and the evening ahead, when his intercom buzzed. "Yes, Beverly?" he asked.

"The lunch delivery is here. Shall I show them to the conference room?"

"Yes please," he replied warmly.

Just then, James, his Senior design architect, poked his head into the office. "Sorry to interrupt, Troy. Just wanted to check if you'd like me to present the November project updates during the meeting and touch on the January project?"

LOVE GOD'S WAY

Troy considered for a moment before responding. "Let's go over November since it's right around the corner, but we'll hold off on January for now. No need to overwhelm everyone before the Thanksgiving holidays," he added with a chuckle.

"Got it, boss," James said with a grin.

As James left, Troy smiled, thinking about his plans to announce James as a partner in the firm. James, a Senior Architect and a loyal team member since the firm's inception, was more than deserving of the promotion—an exciting change slated for the new year.

The staff meeting proceeded smoothly, with Troy reviewing the year's completed projects and expressing his gratitude for his team. "We may be a mid-sized firm, but the work we produce is nothing short of excellence. I'm beyond proud to call us not just a team but a family," he said sincerely.

His light-hearted comment about late nights and weekend deadlines being handled "better than a big firm ever could" drew laughter from the room, lightening the mood.

Naomi, the office manager, presented the project calendar for the remainder of the year. She outlined the timeline for the November project, expected to wrap by early December, and reminded the team to submit vacation requests by November 15. James then detailed the tasks and deadlines for the upcoming projects, ensuring everyone was aligned.

As the meeting concluded, the team enjoyed their catered lunch, laughing and chatting about work and life. At 3:30, Troy stood and announced, "You've all earned an early start to the weekend. Go home and enjoy the rest of your day—with pay, of course!"

The team cheered, gathering their belongings as they thanked him on their way out. Once the office was empty, Troy took a final walkthrough, ensuring everything was cleaned and locked up before heading home.

By 4 PM, Troy was back at his place, preparing for the evening. Excitement and a sense of calm settled over him as he thought about seeing Love and spending time together in worship. Their church date was more than an outing; it was another step toward building a faith-centered relationship.

Troy arrived at Love's house promptly at 6 p.m., dressed in a crisp button-down shirt and slacks. When Love opened the door, he couldn't help but smile. She looked radiant in her elegant yes modest dress and matching pea coat, her hair framing her face perfectly.

"You look beautiful," he said sincerely.

"Thank you," she replied with a shy smile. "And you clean up nicely yourself."

They shared a warm laugh before heading out. The drive to the church was filled with easy conversation, the anticipation of the evening ahead building between them.

Once they arrived, they met up with Jasmine and her husband Darryl who stood close to the entrance waiting on them. Love walked up and hugged Jasmine and Darryl. She turned to Troy and smiled. Jasmine and Darryl, this is Troy she paused and smiled, my Boaz. Jasmine grinned big, reached out and hugged Troy then Darryl shook Troy's hand. "Nice to meet you both", replied Troy with a smile. Troy grabbed Love's hand, and they followed Jasmine and Darryl into the service.

LOVE GOD'S WAY

The service was powerful, with a spirit-filled sermon on walking in faith and trusting God's timing. As they worshiped together, Love felt a deep connection not just with Troy but also with the shared purpose they seemed to have. At the end of service, the pastor invited those who needed prayer and also a special prayer for couples, Troy gently squeezed her.

"Would you like to go up?" he asked softly.

She nodded, and they walked hand in hand to the altar. As the pastor prayed over them, Love felt tears welling in her eyes. It was as if God was confirming that this relationship had His blessing.

Jasmine watched her best friend with her new man get prayer from her pastor and she was overwhelmed. Thank you, God, and bless the union, she prayed quietly.

After the service, they stayed a little longer, chatting with Jasmine and Darryl and other attendees and even taking a moment to pray together privately before heading back to her home.

"This was a perfect way to start the weekend," Love said as they pulled into her driveway.

"I couldn't agree more," Troy replied. "I'll see you in the morning for our day together."

Troy walked Love to her door. Thank you for the invitation, this service was a blessing, Troy said intently. Absolutely, spending everyday together doing God will is what I look forward to, she said. Same here, Troy responded. He grabbed her hand and kissed it softly, good night my beautiful lady, see you in the morning. Okay, handsome let me know when you make it home, please. Of course, Troy said looking back as he walked to his truck.

Love stepped inside and stood against the door, whew God I know this is you and I am enjoying this journey and this feeling.

After a long shower, Love journaled then lay in bed with a smile as she drifted off to sleep.

On Saturday morning, Love got up smiling, happy and full of joy excited for the day. She put on her upbeat playlist, dancing around the house getting ready for the day. The October weather was cool yet extremely sunny, nice weather for an outside picnic. After getting ready she grabbed her bag and a blanket. As she headed toward her front room her doorbell rang.

Troy arrived at Love's house at 10. He got out the truck and moved swiftly to her door. He rang her doorbell and waited at her door. She came out with a blanket as a contribution to the picnic. He chuckles. "What", Love asks with a smile? "You are definitely my better half, because I actually forgot the blanket but you knew", he chuckles even harder.

She giggles "I just figured you may forget and I wanted to contribute something to our picnic, even if you had bought one I still would have bought this one too. This is what happens when you begin to become one with someone". She smiled as he opened the door for her.

They headed to a nearby park with a beautiful lake. They arrived noticing that it was just one other car in the parking area. As they walked through the park, Love noticed in the middle of the open field there was a set-up of a clear large bubble tent with a picnic set up inside. She smiled and asked, "is that for us?" "Yes" Troy said with a huge grin. He let her enter the picnic area first after removing her shoes. There was already a blanket and throw pillows. The food was set up and was beautifully plated with fruit, pasta salad, deviled eggs, sandwiches, water, juice, and lemonade.

Right away, Troy pulls out a small devotional book.

"I thought we could take a few minutes to reflect and pray together," he said.

She smiled, touched by his thoughtfulness. "I'd love that."

As they read the devotion and prayed, Love felt her affection for Troy deepen. He wasn't just a man she enjoyed spending time with—he was a man who genuinely shared her values and faith and always keeps God at the front of what they do.

After the devotion they watched as more people arrived and laughed at the children playing. Love giggled as she recounted how she once climbed a neighbor's apple tree to rescue a stray cat, only to need rescuing herself. Troy chuckled at the mental image. "So you were caring and tried to be brave," he teased.

"Umm more like a little reckless," she admitted, laughing.

Troy shared a story of his own about trying to build a treehouse with his cousins, which ended in disaster when the makeshift ladder they built collapsed after they climbed up in the tree. "We spent more time arguing over who got to be in charge than actually building anything, then getting trapped and who was at fault," he said, laughing.

"Sounds like you were destined to be a leader, even as a kid," Love remarked, her eyes twinkling with admiration.

After their lunch, they decided to play a game of bible trivia then frisbee on the grassy field near the picnic area. Love surprised Troy with her competitive streak, darting across the field with surprising agility. "You didn't tell me you were an athlete!" Troy called out as she made a dash to catch the frisbee.

"Just full of surprises," she said, tossing it back with a grin.

As the sun began to climb higher in the sky, they rented a paddleboat and ventured out onto the calm lake. The gentle ripples of the water reflected the vibrant hues of the sunset, painting a picturesque scene around them.

Troy took the lead, pedaling the boat while Love leaned back, her hand skimming the water. "This is perfect," she said softly, looking out at the horizon.

Troy glanced at her, his expression tender. "It really is. I love the water and being here with you makes it all special."

Love felt her cheeks flush as her heart swelled at his words.

They sat in a comfortable silence, letting the moment settle. It was cool but really sunny and there was no wind. The world felt still, as if time itself had paused just for them. Taking in the moment together they set for a while humble at God's beautiful nature.

With their paddle boat adventure complete, they returned to the picnic bubble, inside they sat back. Love broke the silence. "You know Troy, you are the first man who has ever done anything like this for me and I am so thankful for your love and the effort you always put forth to show me how much you care. I am grateful for moments like these—where it's just us, His creation, and His presence."

They stayed there for a while longer and at around 2 pm Troy began to pack up and clean what he could. About 5 minutes later the event planner, Kim, arrived and advised that she would finish but thanked him for his help. Troy and Love thanked them for such an amazing set up and great food. He gave her a nice tip, grabbed Love's hand and they headed back to the truck.

Troy did not want the day to end so quickly and suggested that they go bowling at AMF lanes. Troy wanted to see more of her competitive side. He enjoyed watching her be so athletic.

As they headed to the bowling alley Love told Troy how she played volleyball and ran track in high school. He laughed and shared that he also ran track and played basketball. They got to the bowling alley and played and laughed like they were kids. They played several games showing their competitive sides.

They left around 5 pm and decided to go to Charleston Crab House for dinner. They enjoyed their meal on the patio eating great food and watching the boats and enjoying each other's company.

They ended the day by sitting on the pier outside the restaurant watching as the sun began to set, the sky painted in shades of orange and pink.

It was a little before 8 pm and they headed back to Love's home hand in hand yet in beautiful silence. They got back to Love's home as Troy walked her to her door that evening, he took her hand and said, "I've had the best day with you, Love. But I always have a great time so this is no different. Thank you for sharing it with me." "Awww Troy me too," she replied. He gently grabbed her and gave her a warm embrace. He slowly let her go. Kissed her forehead and stepped back on the steps.

"Goodnight handsome, please let me know when you make it home."

"Goodnight, beautiful see you in the morning" he lingered as she walked inside then headed to his truck.

On Sunday morning, Troy arrived early, around 830, ready to head to his church. She went to the door, "Hey babe, she said smiling softly. Would you like to come in since we have about 30-45 minutes before we have to leave?" He stepped inside and closed the door. "I just finished making coffee. Would you like some?" "Yes please", he responded.

"Love", he said her name inquisitively. "Yes", she said as she turned around. He smiled, first of all you look stunning. She looked down at her dress, she smiled and said thank you. He returned the smile, and second umm did you call me babe? She giggled, yes I did. Is that okay, I mean I have already told you I love you? He stepped close to her looking her in her eyes, yes you did and it is all beautiful to hear coming from your lips. I just wanted to hear you confirm that I heard what I heard. They both chuckled.

They enjoyed their coffee together and went through some options for lunch after church. As Love excused herself to go finish getting dressed Troy looked around. He saw that she had already started putting up her Christmas decorations with most of it referencing Jesus Christ and his birth. He was so inspired by her set up.

"Beautiful", he said. "What is that?", Love said as she walked up behind him. "You" he said with a huge grin as he turned to face her. "You hadn't even seen me when you said beautiful," she responded. "I know, " he said with a grin, "but my goodness you are, and you went from 5 foot to 6 foot with those heels," he said laughing. "Haha" she replied with a giggle, "I am 5 '4 and yes the heels did take me to right around 5' 11 or 6 ft but still shorter than you sir". He looked right at her. "That is true since I am 6 '2", he replied. "My lady is short". "Yes, I am babe but it's okay you love my height". "I do love you", he said, grabbing her hand as they headed out the door to church.

They got to his church and he glanced at Love. "Are you nervous my love", he asked? She looked at him with a nervous grin. "Yes a little, how did you know," she asked? "Because you play with your hands when you are nervous. I told you I pay attention to you, my Love. You are with me you will be okay; I got you beautiful," he said as he opened the door for her to exit the truck.

As they walked in they were greeted by the church greeters. They smiled and spoke to other attendees on the way to their seats. Troy introduced Love to multiple people including someone of the mothers of the church. He also introduced her to a few of his friends and family members, who were all eager to meet the woman who he has been spending so much time with. She was surprised but elated that they knew who she was. She was introduced to many others after service including his parents and siblings. Love was nervous but over excited to meet them.

The service was uplifting, and Troy felt a surge of pride as Love actively participated, singing along and engaging with the sermon.

After church, they went to Love's favorite restaurant, a cozy spot known for its soulful Southern Country cooking. With their plates of fried chicken, greens, rice and gravy and cornbread, they talked about the service and how great his friends, family and church family treated her.

"Love," Troy said as they finished their meal, "this weekend has been amazing. I feel like I'm learning so much about you, and everything I'm learning just makes me want to know you more."

She smiled, feeling the same way. "Me too, Troy. It feels... different with you. In a good way. A Godly way."

He reached across the table and gently took her hand in his. "That's because it is," Troy said, his eyes meeting hers with unwavering sincerity. "And I'm thankful that His will for me includes you."

Love felt her heart swell at his words, her cheeks flushing with warmth. She hesitated for a moment before speaking, her voice soft but steady. "Troy, how would you feel about meeting my parents?"

A smile spread across his face, and without a second of hesitation, he replied, "I'd love to. Anytime you're ready, just let me know."

Her heart fluttered at his response, and she smiled back. "Today," she said, squeezing his hand gently. "I know it is last minute but it would be great for them to meet the man that makes me so happy!"

He smiled, "yes it would be an honor for me to meet my future family."

Troy parked the truck in front of Love's family home, a quaint, cozy house adorned with twinkling Christmas lights and a wreath on the door. Love glanced over at him, her nerves evident in the way she clutched her coat.

"Relax," Troy said with a reassuring smile. "If they are anything like you, I know I'll love them, and you know they will love me."

She exhaled, laughing softly. "You're so confident and I love it. Just wait until my dad starts grilling you."

Troy chuckled. "I'm ready for it. I promise."

Inside, the aroma of cinnamon and freshly baked cookies greeted them. Love's mom, Patricia, was bustling around the kitchen, her apron dusted with flour, while Joy, her younger sister, sat cross-legged on the couch, scrolling through her phone.

"Hey everyone, we are here," Love said, her voice a mix of excitement and nervous anticipation as she stepped into the cozy living room with him by her side.

When her parents looked up from what they were doing. She smiled; everyone this is Troy."

Her dad set down the newspaper he'd been reading, rising to his feet. His expression was serious but kind, his presence commanding yet approachable. "So, you're the young man Love's been talking about," he said, his tone steady, his eyes carefully studying Troy.

"Yes, sir," Troy replied with a respectful nod, extending his hand for a firm handshake. "It's an honor to meet you, Mr. Wilson."

Her dad grasped his hand, the strength in his grip unmistakable. "Troy, huh? Well, welcome. We've heard quite a bit about you."

Love's mom stepped forward, her warm smile immediately setting Troy at ease. "It's so nice to finally meet you, Troy," she said, pulling him into a quick, welcoming hug before he could react. "Love's been smiling nonstop since she met you."

"Mom!" Love protested, her cheeks flushing, but she was smiling too.

Troy chuckled softly, glancing at Love with a look of quiet affection. "She's amazing," he said, his voice sincere.

As introductions continued, Love's younger sister stood up, her energy vibrant. "You must be Troy!" she exclaimed, her eyes wide with curiosity. "I'm Joy, the cool one in the family. Nice to meet you."

Troy laughed, shaking her hand with mock seriousness. "Nice to meet you too, Joy. I'll take your word for it."

The room filled with laughter, and the initial tension melted away, replaced by the comfortable warmth of family.

As everyone settled into the living room, the conversation turned light and easy. Love, her mom and sister started discussing Christmas plans, reminiscing about past traditions and sharing ideas for the upcoming holiday season.

Troy, noticing a moment of quiet from Frank, Love's dad, Troy leaned over and spoke softly. "Sir, may I have a moment to talk privately?"

Frank raised an eyebrow but nodded. "Sure, let's step outside."

They moved to the back porch, where the crisp December air was cool but not biting. Troy hesitated for a moment, then took a deep breath. "Sir, I know we haven't known each other long, but I wanted to share what's on my heart. Love is... well, she's incredible. Her faith, her kindness, her heart—it's all I've ever prayed for in a partner. I'd like your blessing to ask for her hand in marriage."

Frank studied him for a moment, his face unreadable. "You seem like a good man, Troy. And from what I've heard, you treat my daughter with the respect and love she deserves. But marriage is a big step. Are you ready for the commitment it takes to lead a family, to keep God at the center of it all?"

"Yes, sir," Troy said firmly. "I've prayed about this, and I believe God has led me to Love. I'm committed to loving her the way Christ loves the church, to supporting her dreams, and to building a life together rooted in faith."

Frank smiled, his eyes softening. "That's what I needed to hear. You have my blessing, son. Welcome to the family."

Troy's heart swelled with gratitude as he shook his future father-in-law's hand. "Thank you sir, Troy said. Frank noticed Troy's sigh of relief, so he put a hand on his shoulder, "It didn't take me long to know

Love's mother was the one either. When you know you know." Troy felt relieved that Mr. Wilson didn't think that he was moving too fast.

As Troy and Frank stepped back inside, the lively chatter and laughter from the women in the living room filled the house. Love glanced up, her smile softening when she saw Troy. "Everything okay?" she asked, her gaze flicking curiously between him and her dad. Troy took a moment to simply admire her, silently thanking God for the incredible woman who had captured his heart.

"Perfect," Troy said, his voice steady but his heart racing with the secret he now carried.

Patricia beckoned them over. "Come on, guys. We're debating whether we should stick to our usual Christmas traditions or try something new this year. What do you think, Troy?"

Troy smiled as he took a seat beside Love, her hand instinctively finding his. "Well, I'm a fan of traditions, especially if they bring everyone together. What's one of your favorites?"

Love's sister, Joy, chimed in, her tone playful. "Oh, we always have matching pajamas on Christmas Eve. Dad pretends he hates it, but he secretly loves it."

Frank grumbled good-naturedly. "Let's not ruin my reputation, now."

Everyone laughed, and the conversation meandered through stories of past Christmases like the time the tree fell over just hours before their guests arrived or the year Love baked cookies that were so hard they nearly broke her dad's teeth but he still tried to eat them.

Amid the warmth and laughter, Troy felt a deep sense of belonging. These moments, filled with love and togetherness, felt like a glimpse of the future he hoped to build with Love.

As the evening started to come to a close, Troy helped Frank carry a few chairs back to the garage. As they returned to the house, Love and her mom were tidying up the kitchen, their laughter drifting into the hallway.

As Troy and Love said their goodnights to Love's family, Troy slipped his hand into Love's as he walked to her side to open the door to let her slide into the truck. "Thank you for tonight," he said quietly. "Your family is amazing."

Love tilted her head, studying him. "You're amazing for jumping right in with them. I was worried Dad might scare you off."

"Not a chance," Troy said with a grin, leaning in, he kissed her forehead.

As they drove back to Love's home, their conversation flowed easily, filled with gratitude for the time they'd spent together and anticipation for what was to come. As they stepped out into the crisp night air slowly walking to her front door, Troy's heart felt full. He glanced over at Love, his resolve strengthening. He was certain—tonight had confirmed it. He was going to spend the rest of his life loving her, just as God had planned.

And soon, he'd ask her the question that would change everything.

"Thank you for an amazing weekend and going with me to my parents' home," she said softly.

"The pleasure was all mine, and I enjoyed meeting your family. I think they like me" he replied with a smile.

With a warm smile and a lingering look, they said their goodnights, already looking forward to the next time they'd see each other.

CHAPTER 11

Every day with Troy growing in love was nothing short of magical. Love found herself growing increasingly confident in the love blossoming between her and Troy. She no longer hesitated to invite him over to her place, and she felt at ease visiting his home as well, something that once felt daunting due to her guarded nature. But Troy had a way of making her feel safe and cherished, creating a beautiful sense of security. With him, she could be her authentic self, free from judgment, and their connection only deepened because of it.

Troy, on his part, was utterly captivated by Love. Every moment spent with her reaffirmed how much he admired and adored her. He found himself missing her terribly on the rare days their busy schedules kept them apart. On those days, Face Timing her to see her radiant smile became his favorite remedy.

November arrived with its usual warmth but quickly transitioned into crisp, cool days. For Love, autumn was her favorite season, a time of vibrant colors, cozy sweaters, and the beauty of falling leaves. Troy, busy with a major project at work, still made it a priority to carve out time for Love. He couldn't imagine a week without seeing her and would often plan thoughtful outings for them to share.

This was the first Saturday of November and the leaves painted Charleston in shades of red, orange, and gold, Troy called Love with an idea. "Hey, how do you feel about doing the fall tours today? Maybe we can go for a ride afterward," he suggested.

"Anything I can do with you, I'm all in," Love said with a playful grin.

"Perfect. I'll leave in about 20 minutes to pick you up."

"Okay, babe. I'll be ready," she replied, her excitement evident.

It was a quarter to 12 and Troy arrived earlier than expected, pulling into Love's driveway with a warm smile. Love opened the door, ready with her bag in hand. "You're early," she teased, giggling.

"But it seems you're ready, my love," he quipped, chuckling. "I thought I'd be waiting a little."

"Have I ever made you wait?" she teased back, stepping into his embrace.

"No, you haven't," he admitted with a laugh.

Their day began with the Charleston Preservation Society's fall tours. They strolled hand in hand through historic gardens, marveled at the stately residences, and admired the intricate architecture of the old buildings.

"These homes are incredible," Love said, her eyes shining as she took in the details.

Troy nodded in agreement. "The architecture is beautifully crafted. It's amazing how much history is preserved here."

As they strolled, they came to the last few buildings on the tour, they came across a house that looked like it had been transformed into a beautifully crafted museum. Love stopped in her tracks, her eyes lighting up as she admired the vintage charm of the building.

"This place," she said, her voice filled with awe, "it looks like it's straight out of a 1950s love story. It's absolutely stunning."

Troy smiled, leaning closer and lowering his voice to a whisper. "Guess what?"

"What?" she asked, turning to face him, curiosity sparkling in her eyes.

"My company and I were the architects for this building," he said, a hint of pride in his tone.

Her eyes widened in disbelief. "No way! Are you serious?"

He nodded, chuckling at her reaction. "Yes, ma'am. This building is only about five years old. They reached out with the description of what they wanted it to look like and this is what we drew for them. They were absolutely in awe without creativeness and how we captured exactly what they wanted. It was one of our very first projects, and when they added it to the tour, we couldn't believe it."

Love turned back to the building, taking it in with fresh eyes. "That's absolutely amazing, Troy. You're an incredible architect. This is beautiful!"

Her admiration warmed Troy's heart as he gazed at her. "Hearing you say that means the world to me," he said, squeezing her hand.

She smiled up at him, her voice soft. "You're so talented, babe. I'm proud of you."

They lingered for a moment, sharing the joy of the moment, before continuing their walk, the admiration for each other growing with every step.

After the tour, they made their way to the center of town, walking along cobblestone streets lined with quaint shops. The air was filled with the scent of cinnamon and cider from nearby cafes.

As they approached a charming, cottage-like building, Troy stopped looking at the building. He and Love stepped inside as a couple passed them swiftly, exiting the building and smiling and holding hands.

Troy turned to her with a wide smile. "We're here for the carriage ride," he said casually.

The gentleman in charge stepped forward, glancing at his clipboard. "Mr. Hayes?"

"Yes, sir," Troy replied.

"Wonderful! You're right on time," the man said with a chuckle. He led them to a beautifully adorned carriage waiting nearby.

Love's eyes widened and her mouth dropped in surprise as she realized what Troy had planned. "A carriage ride?" she exclaimed, her voice full of delight. "I thought you meant a ride around town in your truck! This is amazing, Troy. Thank you!" She threw her arms around him in a tight hug.

Troy laughed, kissing her forehead. "Anything for you, my love."

The carriage ride was perfect. Although November brought a chill to the air, there was no wind, making it a crisp yet comfortable evening. The carriage was thoughtfully equipped with a cozy blanket for their laps and a small, attached heater, though they didn't need it. The ride offered breathtaking views of the town's fall colors, the sound of the horse's hooves adding a rhythmic charm to the atmosphere.

Love snuggled closer to Troy, her head resting on his shoulder as they rode through the scenic streets. She felt a deep sense of gratitude for moments like these—simple yet profound.

"Troy," she whispered, "this is perfect."

He looked down at her, his eyes warm. "You make everything perfect, Love."

They rode in comfortable silence, the kind that only comes when two people feel completely at ease with each other, letting the beauty of the season and their growing love speak volumes.

As the carriage gently rolled along the cobblestone streets, Love and Troy soaked in the picturesque views around them. The vibrant hues of autumn leaves adorned the trees, and the golden light of the setting sun bathed everything in a warm, ethereal glow.

Love leaned slightly out of the carriage, her eyes sparkling as she admired the scenery. "This is absolutely magical," she whispered, her voice filled with wonder.

Troy smiled, watching her take it all in. "It really is," he said, his tone soft and genuine.

The sun continued its slow descent, casting long shadows over the town and illuminating the charming architecture in shades of amber and rose. The clip-clop of the horse's hooves and the faint rustling of leaves created a soothing soundtrack to their ride.

As the carriage ride came to an end, the soft glow of the last bit of sunlight blanketed the town. The driver gently pulled the reins, bringing the horses to a stop in front of a charming lamppost that cast a warm golden light over the cobblestone street.

Troy stepped out first, turning back to offer his hand to Love. She accepted it with a smile, stepping down gracefully from the carriage.

"Thank you so much," Troy said to the driver, slipping him a generous tip. The driver tipped his hat and smiled. "My pleasure, sir. You two make quite the pair."

Love glanced back at the carriage, her eyes still twinkling with excitement. "This was incredible, Troy. I don't even know how to thank you."

He pulled her gently into his arms, looking deeply into her eyes. "Seeing you this happy is all the thanks I need," he said, his voice steady and sincere.

They stood there for a moment, the cool autumn air wrapping around them as the stars began to dot the night sky. Love rested her head against Troy's chest, feeling the steady rhythm of his heartbeat.

"This entire day has been like something out of a dream," she murmured.

Troy kissed the top of her head and smiled. "And it's only the beginning, my Love."

Hand in hand, they began to walk, leaving behind the enchanting carriage ride but carrying with them the magic of the evening and the promise of even more beautiful moments to come.

As they drove back to Love's home, the car was filled with the soft hum of the radio and the warmth of their conversation. The crisp autumn air outside was a contrast to the cozy atmosphere inside, where they shared laughter and talked about the upcoming holidays.

"I was thinking," Troy began, glancing at Love with a smile, "how about we spend our first Thanksgiving with my family this year? It would mean a lot to them—and to me."

Love nodded, her eyes lighting up. "That sounds wonderful. I'd love to spend Thanksgiving with your family. And for Christmas, how about we host everyone at my place? My parents and sister would enjoy it, and it would give us all a chance to be together."

Troy's face broke into a grin. "That's perfect. I can help you set everything up. Between your family's energy and our mom's cooking, it's going to be a holiday to remember."

Love laughed softly; her heart warmed at how easily their lives seemed to intertwine. "I can already imagine the house filled with laughter and the smell of cinnamon and pine. It'll be so special."

Troy reached over and took her hand, his fingers intertwining with hers. "Special is an understatement when I get to share it with you."

They continued to plan, talking about favorite dishes, family traditions, and how they'd make this holiday season unforgettable. By the time they pulled up to Love's house, their excitement for the weeks ahead had grown, and their bond felt even stronger.

As Troy walked her to the door, he smiled. "I'm really looking forward to this. Thank you for letting me be a part of your world."

Love turned to him, her expression tender. "Thank you for making it so easy to say yes and be a part of yours."

With a soft kiss on the forehead, they parted ways, both feeling grateful for the joy and love that surrounded their budding relationship.

******

Thanksgiving morning dawned crisp and bright as Love smoothed down her sweater, taking a steady breath. She glanced at herself in the mirror, adjusting the simple gold necklace Troy had given her. Love had already met Troy's family during church, but it was still both exciting and nerve-wracking. This would be longer than a meet and greet, but Troy's reassurances the night before replayed in her mind: *"They're going to love you, Love."*

"Ready again?" Troy asked as he stepped into the room, looking effortlessly handsome in a dark gray sweater that complimented his eyes.

Love turned, her smile nervous but genuine. "I'm ready babe," she said." *I should not be this nervous since I have met them*, she thought.

They arrived at Troy's parents' home just after noon. The house was bustling with energy—laughter and the savory aroma of turkey and spices greeted them as they walked in. The warmth of the family home immediately put Love at ease.

Troy's mom was the first to greet her, pulling her into a tight hug. "So, happy to meet you again and actually get to talk to you, we've heard so much about you!" she exclaimed, her smile radiant. "Troy hasn't stopped talking about you."

Love blushed, glancing at Troy, who simply grinned. "It's so nice to meet you, Mrs. Hayes," Love said warmly.

"Oh, please, call me Diane," Troy's mom insisted. "And this is Troy's dad, Paul Sr."

Paul Sr. held out his hand. "Welcome to the family," he said, his deep voice kind and sincere. She bypassed his hand and gave him a hug.

As Love was reintroduced to Troy's siblings, nieces, and nephews, she felt a sense of belonging start to grow. Everyone was kind, teasing Troy in a way that made her laugh and feel like part of their traditions already.

During the meal, the family held hands as Paul Sr. led them in prayer, thanking God for His blessings and the gift of family. Love couldn't help but glance at Troy as his deep "Amen" echoed through the room, her heart swelling with gratitude.

Conversation flowed easily over plates piled high with turkey, stuffing, and sweet potato casserole. Love shared stories of her own family's holiday traditions, laughing as Troy's younger brother, Paul Jr., jokingly challenged her to a pumpkin pie-eating contest.

After dinner, while the younger kids played outside, Love helped Diane clear the table.

"You've made quite an impression," Diane said, her tone light but meaningful.

Love paused, glancing at her. "I hope so. Your family has been so welcoming—it means a lot to me."

Diane smiled, placing a hand on Love's arm. "Troy's always been steady, but I can tell he's... different with you. Happier. You bring out something beautiful in him. That's all a mother could ask for."

Love felt her cheeks warm. "He's a blessing to me too."

Meanwhile, Troy had taken Paul Sr. aside to share his plans. "Dad, I wanted to let you know I'm planning to ask Love to marry me. I've already spoken to her dad, but your advice means a lot to me."

Paul Sr. studied his son for a moment before nodding. "You've always had a good head on your shoulders, Troy. If you're sure, and you've prayed about it, then I think Love's a wonderful choice. She'll fit right in with this crazy family of ours."

Troy smiled, relieved. "Thanks, Dad."

Later, as the evening wound down, Troy and Love sat on the back porch, the distant laughter of family carrying through the crisp night air. Love rested her head on Troy's shoulder, feeling a deep sense of peace.

"Your family is amazing," she said softly.

"They're even better with you here," Troy replied, lacing his fingers with hers.

Love smiled, the warmth of the day filling her heart. Thanksgiving had always been about gratitude, and this year, she had more to be thankful for than ever.

******

November finished swiftly and smoothly. December seemed to fly by in a blur of joy and festivity. Between planning and spending time with each other's families, it was shaping up to be one of Love's favorite holiday seasons yet. Her home had been fully decked out in Christmas decorations since before Thanksgiving—a tradition she cherished. Christmas was her absolute favorite time of year, and with her work projects wrapped up her vacation started November 20th, every day felt like a celebration.

She spent her days surrounded by holiday cheer, splitting her time between Troy, his family, and her own. It was a season of love, laughter, and gratitude, and everything in Love's world felt just right.

Meanwhile, Troy had also wrapped up his last major project at work. To close out the year, he decided to turn their final work meeting into a Christmas party, setting a festive tone for his team. That Friday, the office was abuzz with excitement, as everyone arrived in their holiday attire, ready to celebrate the season.

Troy stood at the front of the room, smiling warmly as he began the meeting. "Once again, our clients are thrilled with our work," he announced. "We completed the project due on November 10th well ahead of schedule—before the start of November. That's incredible teamwork, and I couldn't be prouder."

The room erupted into applause and cheers.

Troy turned to Naomi. "Naomi, is there anything left on the calendar for the year?"

Naomi scanned her notes. "No, sir, nothing's left for this year. I just want to confirm that several staff members have requested vacations through the start of the new year."

Troy nodded and glanced around. "How many of you are planning to take some time off?"

Several hands shot up, though a few hesitated and slowly lowered theirs. Troy chuckled. "Come on, don't be shy. You all deserve it. All vacation requests are approved. For those who'll be here during the holiday season, we'll be working half-days—no one stays past noon until after New Year's Day."

The room erupted in cheers again, and the mood grew even more celebratory.

Troy held up his hand for quiet. "Before we wrap up, I have two quick announcements. First, I'll be on vacation through the new year, but I'll have my phone on me, so don't hesitate to reach out if you need anything."

He then turned toward James, who was sitting near the front. "Second, James, you've been with me since the very beginning. Your dedication and leadership have been a cornerstone of this firm's success. Today, I'm thrilled to officially offer you a promotion to Partner."

The room fell silent for a moment as James stared at Troy, his mouth agape in shock. "Is that a yes?" Troy teased, grinning.

James finally found his voice, though it came out in a stutter. "Yes—oh, absolutely, yes! Thank you, Troy. Thank you so much."

"You've earned it," Troy said, shaking James's hand firmly. "Your hard work hasn't gone unnoticed. And to everyone here—be ready for more exciting changes in the new year."

The team broke into applause once again, congratulating James and celebrating the moment.

Troy clapped his hands together. "All right, everyone. Let's wrap it up here. Enjoy your weekend, and Merry Christmas!"

As the team began to file out, chatting and laughing, Troy felt a deep sense of fulfillment. The year had been challenging but rewarding, and now he could look forward to the holiday season—and spending it with Love.

It was the Saturday before the week of Christmas. He watched as she cooked dinner for them. He normally helped but at this dinner he was asked to sit in the living room. She told him this dinner she was making was special and he could not assist her this time.

As she glided through the kitchen, he smiled watching her move from counter to stove to refrigerator back to the counter. The aroma of spices filled the air as Love stirred the pot of her special dish, her movements graceful and deliberate. Her curled locs bounced lightly with every step, and her laughter occasionally echoed into the living room when she sang along to her favorite upbeat gospel playlist. Troy leaned back on the couch, smiling to himself, his heart swelling as he watched her. She was a vision-confident, joyful, and entirely at peace. She had handed him the remote to watch whatever he liked on the tv but he was watching exactly what he wanted......Her. He knew that he wanted to spend the rest of his life with her, and it did not take years to know. Once God gave him the confirmation that she was his wife that was all he needed to know but he knew that he wanted her to feel safe and comfortable to be ready for the next steps.

For Troy, the past several months had been a revelation. Love wasn't just the woman he admired; she was the woman God had shown him in quiet whispers during his prayers. Her faith, her kindness, and her determination to live with purpose had captured his heart, and he found himself imagining a lifetime with her—building a home, growing in faith, and creating memories they could tell their children and grandchildren someday.

As Love placed the last touches on their dinner, she turned toward him, catching his gaze. "Hey, no peeking!" she teased, pointing a wooden spoon at him. Her eyes sparkled with mischief, and Troy chuckled.

"Can't help it," he replied, leaning forward. "You're the best show on TV right now."

Love rolled her eyes, but the warmth of his words made her cheeks flush. She had spent the week planning this meal, not because she wanted to impress him, Troy already made her feel like the most cherished woman in the world, but because she wanted to show him just how much he meant to her. Over the months, she had learned to let her guard down, trusting that Troy's love was genuine and unwavering. Tonight, she wanted to celebrate the beautiful journey they were on.

When the table was set, and the meal was ready, she called Troy over. He stood, smoothing out his shirt as he walked into the kitchen. The sight before him took his breath away not just the beautifully arranged table with candles and Love's signature dishes but the glow on her face, the love in her eyes.

"This looks amazing," he said, his voice soft. He reached for her hand and pulled her close, his thumb brushing lightly over her knuckles. "But not as amazing as you."

Love smiled, feeling a mixture of shyness and boldness bubbling up inside her.

Troy's heart raced, the words he had been holding onto bubbling to the surface. He cupped her face gently, his gaze locking with hers.

"Love, I prayed for you," he said, his voice filled with emotion. "And every day of the last six months with you has confirmed what God told me from the start—you are my answered prayer. You're my partner, my best friend, and the woman I want to spend forever with."

Tears brimmed in Love's eyes as she saw the sincerity in his expression. Her heart felt full, as if every piece of her life had led her to this moment. Dinner could wait—this love, this moment, was the feast her heart had longed for.

Troy took a deep breath and stepped back, reaching into his pocket. Love was completely unsuspecting as she watched him, her heart skipped a beat, time seemed to slow, and the air around them felt charged with anticipation. She didn't want to assume what was happening, but her mind raced as she saw his hand emerge, holding a small velvet box.

"Love," Troy began, his voice steady and full of conviction. "From the moment I met you, I knew you were special. But as I've spent these months with you, I've come to see just how extraordinary you are. You're kind, patient, and strong, and your love for God shines so brightly that it draws everyone around you closer to Him—including me."

Love's breath caught as she listened, tears now streaming freely down her face. Troy dropped to one knee, his eyes never leaving hers.

"I've prayed about this, and I know without a doubt that you are the woman God has chosen for me. Love, I want to build a life with you. I want to serve God with you, dream with you, and face every challenge this world throws at us together. Will you do me the honor of being my wife?"

Love's hands flew to her mouth as she let out a soft sob. She could feel the weight of the moment, the sincerity in his voice, and the immense love in his eyes. Her heart overflowed, and she nodded quickly before finding her voice.

"Yes," she whispered, then louder, "Yes, Troy! I'll marry you!"

Troy's face broke into the widest smile she had ever seen as he opened the box, revealing a delicate three stone ring with sparkling diamonds that seemed to catch the light in the room perfectly. He slipped the ring onto her finger, they never discussed ring sizes, but her ring fit perfectly, and it was exactly what she wanted, a three stone was radiant cut.

As Troy rose, Love flung her arms around his neck, holding him tightly. She felt his arms wrapped securely around her, and they both laughed through their tears, unable to contain the joy that filled the room.

The dinner was forgotten for the moment as they stood in the dining room next to the beautiful Christmas tree, holding onto each other and the promise of a lifetime together. Eventually, Troy pulled back just enough to look at her.

"I hope you don't mind," he said, a playful grin tugging at his lips, "but I might've already told my parents and siblings. They're so excited to meet their future daughter and sister-in-law."

Love laughed, her cheeks flushed with happiness and tears. "I don't mind at all. You've already met my family, and they adore you. I guess now we just have to start planning this wedding."

Troy chuckled, pulling her close again. "As long as I get to call you my wife, you can't plan anything you want."

Love leaned her head against his chest, feeling his heartbeat steady and strong beneath her ear. In that moment, she felt the completeness of God's love and the beauty of His timing. She knew their journey wouldn't always be easy, but with Troy by her side and God at the center, she was ready to step into the future with faith and excitement.

After a few moments of holding each other, Troy pulled back slowly and cupped Love's face, tilting her chin so she could meet his gaze. His eyes, filled with adoration, sparkled like the ring now adorning her finger.

"I don't think I've ever been this happy in my entire life," he said softly.

"Me either," Love replied, her voice barely above a whisper. "This feels like a dream, Troy. You—us—everything is so perfect."

Troy nodded his head with a smile, in agreement. God's hand is all over this. I know that, and I know we'll get through anything because He's at the center of it."

Love nodded, a fresh wave of tears welling in her eyes. She had spent so much of her life guarding her heart, unsure if this kind of love was meant for her. But here, with Troy, she felt something she had never known, a love rooted in faith, trust, and purpose.

"Okay," she said, stepping back with a playful grin and brushing her tears away. "We still need to eat before this food gets cold. We have to celebrate this engagement properly!"

Troy laughed, letting her guide him to the table. He held out her chair like the gentleman he had always been, then sat across from her, his eyes never leaving hers. They joined hands and bowed their heads as Love said grace, her voice trembling with emotion as she thanked

God for the meal, the man sitting before her, and the beautiful future ahead of them.

As they ate, their conversation flowed effortlessly, the room filled with so much emotion. They spoke about everything—how Troy had nervously hidden the ring in his coat pocket for weeks, waiting for the right moment, also how he had bought the ring during the first week after they officially began courting. She spoke about how she felt like something was happening but could not place what it was. They laughed, teased, and dreamed together about what the next steps would look like.

"I have to admit," Troy said, leaning back in his chair with a satisfied sigh, "you've completely spoiled me. This dinner was incredible, and now I have a fiancée. I feel like the luckiest man alive."

Love laughed, her cheeks warming. "Well, I don't want to brag, but I am pretty amazing."

Troy chuckled, reaching across the table to take her hand. "That you are. And I can't wait to spend every day reminding you just how amazing you are."

After dinner, they moved to the couch, their plates and glasses left for later. Love snuggled into Troy's side as he wrapped an arm around her, pulling her close. The warmth of the moment surrounded them, a quiet peace settled in as the glow of the Christmas tree lights filled the room.

"I love that we got engaged right before Christmas," Love said, her voice soft. "It feels like the perfect season for something so beautiful."

"It does," Troy agreed. "And it gives us one more reason to celebrate this time of year. I've always loved Christmas, but now it'll mean even more."

Love tilted her head to look up at him. "So...how do you feel about wedding planning? Are you ready for all the decisions, details, and discussions about centerpieces?"

Troy grinned, pressing a kiss on her forehead. "As long as I end up married to you, I'll sit through every conversation about flowers, colors, and whatever else you want. Just tell me the date, and I'll be there."

Love giggled, her heart light. "I'll hold you to that."

They sat in comfortable silence for a while, their hearts full and their minds brimming with thoughts of the future. For Love, the journey to this moment has not always been easy, but now, with Troy by her side, she felt the truth of God's promise: when you trust Him, He brings the right person into your life at the right time.

As they sat together, Love glanced up at Troy, her fingers absentmindedly tracing small patterns on his arm. She took a deep breath, her heart brimming with both excitement and nervousness.

"Troy," she began softly, her voice steady but thoughtful. "I've been thinking about the wedding...about what I'd want it to look like."

Troy turned his attention fully to her, his eyes filled with curiosity and affection. "I'm listening. Tell me everything."

Love smiled, her gaze drifting toward the glow of the Christmas tree lights as she gathered her thoughts. "I don't want anything big or extravagant. That's just not me. I've always dreamed of something simple, intimate, a wedding on the beach. Just us, the waves, and the people who mean the most to us. Close family, a few friends, nothing more."

Troy's face softened as he listened. "That sounds beautiful," he said, his voice low and sincere. "It's perfect, Love. Simple and meaningful, just like you."

She blushed, tucking a strand of hair behind her ear. "And I was thinking...shades of blue for the colors. Something soft and serene, like the ocean and the sky."

"Blue, huh?" Troy grinned. "I can see it now—you in a gorgeous white dress, everyone surrounded by the beauty of the beach, the water sparkling like your eyes." He chuckled, giving her hand a gentle squeeze. "And me, probably sweating in the sun, but loving every second of it."

Love laughed, swatting his arm lightly. "There'll be plenty of shade, I promise! We'll make it comfortable for everyone."

Troy shook his head, his expression serious now. "Love, as long as you're there, I'll be comfortable anywhere. If a beach wedding is your dream, it's my dream too."

Her heart swelled at his words, and she felt a wave of gratitude wash over her. "Thank you, Troy. I just want it to feel like...us, you know? Nothing flashy, just something that reflects who we are and what we value."

Troy nodded, "As long as we keep God at the center, surrounded by people who we love that love us, that's all that really matters."

Love rested her head on his shoulder, feeling a profound sense of peace. "I'm so glad I get to do this with you," she murmured.

"And I'm glad God gave me you," Troy replied, pressing a kiss to the top of her head. "Now, when are we getting started on planning this beach wedding? I can already picture the waves, the sunset, and you walking down the aisle."

Love smiled, her heart soaring at the thought. "Can we enjoy this moment for now," she said, snuggling closer. "We can start planning soon but for tonight, I just want to soak this all in......with you."

Troy tightened his hold on her, his heart full of love and anticipation for the journey ahead. The future was bright, and with God guiding their steps, he knew they could face anything together.

CHAPTER 12

After the excitement of the proposal settled, Love and Troy decided to share their news during the Christmas gathering. Love's home, already decorated with twinkling lights, a tall Christmas tree adorned in silver and gold in the living room and a tree laced with gold and white in the dining room, and the faint scent of cinnamon and pine, became the perfect gathering place.

Both families had already eagerly accepted the invitation back in October, thrilled to meet the people who had become so important in Love and Troy's lives. The couple spent the next few days before Christmas planning every detail in addition to what they discussed after their carriage ride, from the menu to the decor, to ice breakers. Love wanted everything to feel cozy and welcoming, and Troy made sure to remind her not to stress—everyone was already excited just to be together.

Christmas

On Christmas morning, the house was filled with the scent of the breakfast cinnamon rolls baking in the oven. The first to arrive were Love's parents, who immediately embraced Troy like a son. Her mother, Patricia, clasped his hands and smiled warmly. "Merry Christmas, it is so good to see you," she said.

"Merry Christmas, Mrs. Wilson," Troy said with his trademark sincerity. "Love has been just as much of a blessing to me."

Patricia laughed. "Call me Patricia, dear. We're practically family now!"

Soon after, Troy's parents arrived, along with his two sisters and younger brother. Love greeted each of them with a warm hug, her nervousness melting away at their kind smiles and genuine enthusiasm.

"Merry Christmas, Love," Troy's mother, Diane, said, her voice soft and affectionate.

Love blushed, squeezing Diane's hand. "Merry Christmas it is so good to see you again."

Troy and Love stood before their families. They thanked everyone for coming and how excited they were for everyone to meet each other. Troy and Love began to introduce their families to each other. As soon as the introductions were over they immediately shared the news of their engagement with everyone. Love slipped her ring on struggling to keep it off before they made their announcement. Everyone was so excited, both mothers running to them hugging them and in tears.

Patricia said to Troy, "I am so happy! I can absolutely see why Love lights up when she talks about you," she said. "You've been such a blessing to her."

"You've already won us over, Love," Troy's mother, Diane said, her voice soft and affectionate. "Troy hasn't stopped talking about you since the day he met you. It's a joy to finally meet the woman who has his heart."

The siblings were all smiling and talking to each other about how they kept it a secret.

Both fathers standing back next to each other, smiling, discuss how great Troy and Love are together.

As the day unfolded, the two families mingled effortlessly. The living room buzzed with conversation and laughter as they exchanged stories about Love and Troy's childhoods, shared memories of Christmas traditions, and marveled at how seamlessly their lives were coming together.

Troy's sisters, Elaine and Naomi, took to Love immediately. They sat with her near the fireplace, peppering her with questions about the engagement. Joy and Paul Jr. walked over and chimed in about the engagement. The siblings continued to chat after Love excused herself, talking to each other about young adult social issues and doing Tik Tok dances.

Love stood glancing across the room where Troy was chatting with their fathers. He caught her eye and winked, making her heart flutter.

The mothers were in the kitchen preparing to bring out hot cocoa and cookies.

Everyone gathered around the tree, mugs of hot cocoa in hand and eating cookies, as they exchanged gifts. It wasn't just about the presents, though—the warmth and joy in the room made it clear this was about celebrating the love that had brought them all together.

Troy handed Love a small box wrapped in blue paper. "This one's for you," he said, his voice soft.

Love opened it carefully, revealing a silver bracelet engraved with the words "God's perfect timing." Her eyes filled with tears as she looked up at him.

"I couldn't have asked for a more perfect gift," she whispered.

"It's a reminder," Troy said, his hand covering hers, "that His timing brought us here, and it'll carry us through every step of our journey."

That afternoon, after a delicious dinner and heartfelt prayers of gratitude, the families sat around the fireplace, singing carols and reminiscing about the day.

As Love looked around the room, her heart swelled with joy. God had not only blessed her with Troy but also with the union of two families who already felt like one. It was a Christmas she would never forget—the first of many she and Troy would share as they built their lives together.

The weeks that followed were a whirlwind of joyful planning, more meaningful introductions of the family and friends that could not make it to Christmas festivities. Creating beautiful and cherished memories as Love and Troy prepared for their wedding. True to Love's vision, every detail of their intimate sunset beach wedding came together beautifully, reflecting their personalities, faith, and the love they shared.

They spent weekends exploring venues along the coast, finally settling on a secluded stretch of beach where the golden hues of sunset met the calm, rolling waves. Love could already picture the scene in her mind: soft shades of blue in the décor, accented with creamy whites and touches of silver, blending seamlessly with the natural beauty of the ocean.

Troy, the supportive fiancé, found himself surprisingly invested in the details. He accompanied Love to floral consultations, cake tastings, and décor appointments, offering his opinion when asked and marveling at how effortlessly she brought everything together.

"I didn't realize planning a wedding could be this much fun," he joked one evening as they sketched out seating arrangements at her dining table.

"That's because we're doing it together," Love replied, smiling warmly at him. "And because it's simple—just the way we want it."

The simplicity extended to their guest list, which included only close family and friends. Over the weeks, the families continued to spend time together getting closer to each other, forming bonds that made their union feel even more special. Love's family adored Troy, praising his kind heart and the way he treated her with unwavering respect. Similarly, Troy's family welcomed Love with open arms, embracing her as one of their own.

"Our families are amazing," Love said after spending an afternoon baking dishes with their mother's and sisters. "It was so fun like we've known each other our entire lives."

The harmony between their families brought an extra layer of joy to the planning process. Both sides pitched in to help where they could, from crafting centerpieces to organizing travel arrangements. Their shared excitement made everything smoother and more meaningful.

Troy and Love spent New Year's Eve in church bringing in the New Year praying and praising God for all the blessings of the previous year. Love asked her family to come to Troy's church with her that night. Troy was thrilled to see both families there, but they did not truly know why until the end. After the altar call to salvation was over the Pastor made a call for anyone who was interested to join the church. It was not a normal request during New Year Eve service however, Love had gone to Pastor Green after their engagement to ask if she could join the church with both her families there during New Year Eve service and he agreed.

After the call to join as everyone looked around Love stepped out and walked to the front of the church. Pastor Green gave her a hug and she turned and faced the audience. Looking at her family, she saw her mom and soon to be mother in love in tears, she looked at Troy and he was also in awe and had tears in his eyes. Pastor Green began "We are so glad you have chosen to join our family of faith. We welcome you with open arms and hearts and pray that you find a pace of belonging and growth here. I would also like to invite Troy Hayes up here to join Ms. Love Wilson. Once he got to the front, he hugged Love tight. He stood beside her as Pastor Green announce their engagement and everyone erupted in applause. "Now church, let's welcome our new member Love Wilson soon to be Hayes to your family." Everyone filed up to the front, including both their families, to hug and shake Love's hand welcoming her to their church family.

As Troy drove to Love's home. He looked at her with the biggest grin. "Babe, I did not know you were even thinking of joining my church." She grinned and squeezed his hand, "I know I wanted to surprise you. I hope you are not upset that I did not share this with you." "Absolutely not babe, this was an amazing surprise, he said." "Great, I want to be where my husband to be is," she said, relieved. Great start to the New Year!

CHAPTER 13

As the weeks turned into months, Love and Troy carved out moments amidst the busyness to focus on their relationship and faith. They attended premarital counseling sessions with Pastor Green, which deepened their understanding of each other and strengthened their spiritual foundation. They prayed together often, seeking God's guidance and giving thanks for the blessings they had been given.

One evening late in June, as they sat on the beach where they would soon say their vows, Troy reached for Love's hand. The setting sun cast a warm glow over the water, and the gentle sound of the waves filled the air.

"You know," Troy said, his voice soft, "this is more than I ever dreamed of. Not just the wedding, but everything—us, our families, the life we're building together."

Love smiled, leaning her head on his shoulder. "It feels like everything is exactly how it's meant to be. God's been so faithful to us, Troy. I'm so excited for what's ahead."

"So am I," he replied, tilting his head to kiss her temple. "I can't wait to see you walking toward me on this very beach, knowing I get to spend forever with you."

Love closed her eyes, letting the moment sink in. In just a couple weeks, this beach would become the backdrop for the start of their new chapter—a chapter filled with love, faith, and the promise of a lifetime together.

Wedding Day

The day of Love and Troy's wedding arrived, graced with clear skies and a soft breeze that carried the scent of saltwater and blooming flowers. It was another beautifully warm day in July, a perfect setting for their intimate sunset beach wedding—a moment they had dreamed of and meticulously planned for months.

Love woke up in a cozy beachfront villa, surrounded by her closest friends and family. The room buzzed with excitement as her bridesmaids, Jasmine, her sister and sisters in love, helped her get ready. The soft shades of blue she had chosen for the wedding colors were reflected in every detail, from the flowy dresses of her bridal party to the ribbons on the bouquets of white roses and baby's breath.

Love's mother, Patricia, carefully adjusted her veil, tears glistening in her eyes.

"You look stunning, sweetheart," she said, her voice thick with emotion. "Troy is going to be speechless." "He sure is Diane agreed."

Love smiled, her own eyes misty. "I can't believe this day is finally here."

Meanwhile, Troy was getting ready in a nearby villa with his dad, father in love and groomsmen, James and Darryl, including his younger brother, Paul Jr. Dressed in a crisp linen suit with a light blue tie, Troy looked out the window at the ocean. The waves lapped gently against the shore, reminding him of the peace and certainty he felt about marrying Love.

"Are you ready for this?" Paul Jr. asked, clapping him on the back.

Troy grinned; his heart was full. "I've been ready since the day I met her."

As the late afternoon sun dipped closer to the horizon, guests gathered on the beach, their seats arranged in neat rows under a canopy of sheer white fabric. A simple wooden arch, adorned with cascading blue hydrangeas and white roses, framed the ocean backdrop. The sound of waves rolling onto the shore created a serene, almost sacred atmosphere.

Troy stood at the altar, his hands clasped in front of him, his heart pounding as he waited for Love.

The music began to play You by Jesse Powell, and everyone rose to their feet. Love appeared; her arm linked with her father's. Her dress was an elegant, flowy gown with delicate lace detailing, perfectly complementing the soft breeze that tugged at her veil. Her smile radiated pure joy, and when her eyes met Troy's, it was as if the world around them faded away.

When she reached him, her father kissed her cheek before placing her hand in Troy's, as the music slowly faded out.

"You look breathtaking," Troy whispered, his voice full of emotion.

"So do you," Love replied, her heart swelling with gratitude for the man standing before her.

The ceremony was simple and heartfelt, centered on their shared faith. Their pastor spoke about the importance of love and commitment, drawing parallels between the strength of their relationship and the unchanging nature of God's love. And keeping God first to stay as uneasily unbroken as a 3-strand cord.

When it was time for their vows, Troy took Love's hands in his.

"Love, from the moment God brought you into my life, I knew you were someone special. You've taught me what it means to love selflessly and to trust fully. I promise to honor you, cherish you, and lead us in faith every day of our lives. I thank God for you, and I vow to love you with all that I am, forever."

Love's voice trembled as she began her vows, her eyes glistening with tears.

"Troy, you are my answered prayer and my greatest blessing. With you, I've found love rooted in faith, patience, and trust. I promise to stand by your side, to encourage you, and to honor the man God has called you to be. I'm so grateful He chose us for each other, and I will always love you."

As they exchanged rings and the pastor pronounced them husband and wife, Troy leaned in for their very first kiss, sealing their union of love to the sound of cheers and applause.

After the ceremony, as their guests mingled and enjoyed light refreshments, Love and Troy stepped away with their photographer for a private photo session. The timing was perfect, the sun was just beginning its descent, casting a warm, golden glow across the sky and water.

The photographer guided them to a spot near the water where the waves gently kissed the shore. Love's dress flowed around her like a dream, and Troy couldn't take his eyes off her.

"Let's start with something candid," the photographer said, smiling. "Just walk along the shoreline and pretend I'm not here."

Love slipped her hand into Troy's, and they strolled barefoot along the sand, laughing softly at an inside joke. The photographer captured their easy, natural connection—the way Troy looked at her as if she were the only person in the world, and the way Love's smile lit up every frame.

As the sun dipped lower, painting the horizon with hues of pink, orange, and gold, the photographer posed them for some more intimate shots.

"Stand close, almost forehead to forehead," she instructed. "Troy, wrap your arms around her waist, and Love, rest your hands on his chest."

The result was breathtaking. The setting sun cast a halo of light around them, and the sparkle in Love's eyes mirrored the glimmer of the waves behind her.

For one shot, the photographer had Love turn her back to Troy as he wrapped his arms around her from behind, both of them looking out at the horizon. The moment felt so peaceful and reflective—perfectly capturing the serenity of their union.

"Now, Troy, pick her up!" the photographer suggested with a grin. Troy laughed and scooped Love into his arms effortlessly, spinning her around as she squealed and laughed. The joy on their faces was infectious, and the photographer snapped the perfect shot with the sun setting behind them.

The final set of photos featured the couple standing under the floral arch, which framed the glowing horizon.

"Troy, lean in and kiss her," the photographer said softly.

As they shared a tender kiss, the camera clicked, immortalizing the moment. The sun dipped just below the horizon, and the sky deepened into shades of lavender and navy, marking the perfect conclusion to the session.

When they returned to the reception, their cheeks were pink from laughter and the sea breeze. Their photographer smiled, showing them a preview of a few shots.

"These are incredible," Love whispered, squeezing Troy's hand.

"They're nothing compared to you," Troy said, brushing a strand of hair from her face.

The photos captured not just the beauty of the setting, but the essence of their love.

The reception was held just a few steps from the ceremony site, under a beautifully decorated tent. String lights twinkled above, and tables were set with blue and white linens, seashell centerpieces, and glowing candles. They sat at the head table to enjoy their ceremony meal with friends and family surrounding them.

Troy's toast was simple yet heartfelt. "Love, you've made me the happiest man alive today. I'm so grateful to everyone here who has supported us, prayed for us, and celebrated with us. But most of all, I'm grateful to God for bringing us together. Here's to a lifetime of love, faith, and adventure."

As Troy finished his heartfelt toast, the soft strains of "Her" by Isaac Carree began to play, drawing murmurs of delight from the guests. With a warm smile, Troy turned to Love, extending his hand.

"May I have this dance, Mrs. Hayes?" he asked, his eyes sparkling.

Love blushed, placing her hand in his. "You may, Mr. Hayes."

He gently led her to the center of the dance floor. As the first lyrics filled the air, Troy pulled her close, his arm wrapping securely around her waist while her hand rested lightly on his shoulder. The romantic melody seemed to weave around them, drawing them into a world where only they existed.

Troy had carefully chosen the song long before their wedding day, knowing its heartfelt lyrics captured everything he felt for Love. As they swayed, he whispered softly in her ear, "Every word in this song is how I feel and how I thank God for you."

Love's eyes shimmered with emotion as she looked up at him. "I love your choice, and I love you."

The photographer moved discreetly around them, capturing the way Love's dress swirled with each step and the way Troy gazed at her, utterly captivated. Guests watched with smiles and happy tears, the love between the couple radiating through the room.

Midway through the dance, Troy leaned in, resting his forehead against hers for a brief moment. It wasn't just a performance; it was a heartfelt expression of their union and the depth of their connection.

As the music softly fades from their first dance to "*Isn't She Lovely*" by Stevie Wonder. Frank knew that it was his queue to grab his daughter's hand.

Love stayed on the floor and switched hands from Troy's to her hand resting in her father's. The melody of a tender ballad filled the air, and Patricia's eyes glistened as he led his daughter in a gentle sway.

"I can't believe my little girl is married," her father said, his voice warm and slightly emotional.

Love smiled, tears threatening to spill. "I wouldn't be here without your love and guidance, Dad. You've been my rock."

He nodded; his voice thick with pride. "And now you have Troy to be your rock. He's a good man, Love. But don't forget, I'm always here if you need me." She nodded with tears in her eyes. She rests her head on her father's shoulder as they continue their father daughter dance.

The song came to an end as Love and her father shared a laugh. Love hugged her father tightly, feeling a surge of gratitude for the man who had always been her protector.

As Love left the dance floor, Troy approached his mother, Diane, and extended his hand with a playful bow. She laughed and joined him, the two swaying together as the next song played, *you are the sunshine of my life*, by Stevie Wonder.

"I'm so proud of you, Troy," Diane said softly. "You've grown into such an incredible man."

"That's because I had you and Dad as an example," Troy replied, his eyes warm. "Thank you for teaching me how to love and lead with faith. Love and I wouldn't be here without that."

Diane's smile grew, and she placed her hand over his. "Cherish her, Troy. Keep God at the center of your marriage, and everything else will fall into place."

As the music transitioned seamlessly, Troy turned to Patricia, Love's mother, and offered his hand. Meanwhile, Love walked over to Diane's husband, Paul Sr., her new father-in-law, who greeted her with a kind smile. They danced as the DJ played; *I'll Be There* by Jackson 5.

Troy and Patricia danced to a lively tune that brought laughter to both of them.

"Thank you for raising such an incredible daughter," Troy said sincerely. "She's everything I've prayed for and more."

Patricia's eyes softened. "And thank you for loving her the way you do. You've brought so much joy to her life, Troy. But remember, marriage isn't always easy. Lean on God, especially in the hard times, and keep choosing each other every day."

"I promise I will," Troy replied, his voice steady. "Thank you for trusting me with her heart."

Paul Sr., Troy's father, led Love in a smooth, graceful dance.

"I'm honored to finally call you my daughter," Paul Sr. said warmly. "Troy chose well."

Love smiled, feeling instantly at ease in his presence. "Thank you, Mr. Hayes. You've raised an amazing man."

"Call me Paul," he said, chuckling. "And thank you for loving my son. Just remember, communication and forgiveness are key. And keep Christ at the center, it's the best advice I can give you."

"I will," Love promised. "I've already learned so much from Troy about faith and love."

As the final notes of The Jackson 5 faded, the DJ invited everyone to join the couple on the dance floor. The transition was seamless, with upbeat music from Sister Sledge singing *We Are Family* inviting laughter and joy as friends and family surrounded Love and Troy.

The reception was in full swing under the softly lit tent, with the sounds of waves in the background and laughter filling the air.

The dance floor came alive with movement and cheer, the couple often spinning apart to dance with their loved ones before finding their way back to each other, their hands and hearts never far apart.

As the music began to slow down, Troy and Love found each other on the dance floor again dancing to *So Into You* by Jac Ross, their families applauding around them. They shared a knowing look, grateful for the wisdom and blessings they'd received from each of their parents. Together, they joined hands and beckoned everyone back to the dance floor, continuing the night's celebration with joy and gratitude for the love that had brought two families together as one.

Everyone danced and laughed with each other through several songs.

As the evening wound down, Love and Troy snuck away and decided to walk barefoot along the shoreline, hand in hand, the moonlight casting a silver glow over the water.

"Today was everything I dreamed of and more," Love said, leaning into him.

"It was perfect," Troy agreed, pulling her close. "And it's just the beginning. I can't wait to spend forever with you."

With the waves lapping at their feet and their hearts full of gratitude, they knew that their journey together was off to the most beautiful start. They went back to their villa to change and pack their luggage for their honeymoon and place it in the car.

They made their way back right as the last song played, Love and Troy stood hand-in-hand, looking out at the twinkling lights strung above and the smiling faces of their loved ones. The evening had been everything they dreamed of filled with love, laughter, and the presence of God in every moment. Now, it was time for the next chapter: their honeymoon.

Guests gathered outside the reception tent, lining the sandy path to the waiting car. Sparklers lit up the night, casting a golden glow on the happy couple as they prepared to leave.

Love had changed into a simple, elegant white dress that flowed as she walked, while Troy had swapped his tie for a more casual, relaxed look. Both wore wide smiles as they made their way through the crowd, waving and laughing as friends and family cheered them on.

"You're glowing," Troy whispered, leaning close as they reached the car.

"It's because I'm with you," Love replied, her voice soft but full of joy.

Before climbing into the car, they turned back to their families, who stood near the entrance waving goodbye. Love's mother blew her a kiss, while Troy's parents gave him a proud thumb-up. The sight of both families united in love and celebration was the perfect send-off.

"Take care of her, Troy!" Love's father called out.

"With all my heart," Troy replied with a smile, opening the car door for Love.

As the car pulled away, Love rested her head on Troy's shoulder, her fingers laced with his. The sound of the sparklers and cheers faded into the background as they looked ahead to their future together.

"Where are we going first?" Love asked, her voice filled with excitement.

Troy grinned. "That's a surprise. But I can promise you that it'll be unforgettable."

Love laughed softly; her heart full. "I don't care where we go, as long as I'm with you."

The couple's destination was filled with multiple stops, where they will spend a couple weeks basking in the beauty of God's creation. Beautiful cities, white sandy beaches, crystal-clear waters, and the promise of uninterrupted time together awaited them. Troy had planned every detail, wanting their first days as husband and wife to be as special as their wedding day.

As the car carried them toward the airport, Love and Troy shared a quiet moment of prayer, thanking God for the incredible blessing of their union and the journey ahead. They knew the honeymoon was just the beginning of a lifetime of adventures together.

When they arrived at the airport, Love turned to Troy with a smile.

"Are you ready for forever?" she asked.

Troy cupped her face and kissed her deeply. "I've never been more ready."

With that, they stepped into their new life together, hearts full of gratitude and love.

Colossians 3:14 - And above all these put on love, which binds everything together in perfect harmony.

ABOUT THE AUTHOR

Blue Kendria Berry is a proud native of Columbia, SC, whose journey has taken her across many places, thanks to her family's deep-rooted military background. A devoted child of Yahweh, she carries a profound passion for His people and the art of storytelling.

Her professional career spans both the legal field and customer service, where her commitment to excellence has always been evident. However, her love for writing began much earlier—back in the 5th grade—when she penned her first book of short stories. Over the years, she continued crafting multiple stories and novellas, eventually writing her first novel in 2010. In 2023, she embarked on this novella, a labor of faith and inspiration, which she proudly completed in December 2024 and published in January 2025.

Beyond writing, Blue is a dynamic entrepreneur. She is the owner of **Blue's Notary Services** and **Beautiful Kreations**, a thriving skincare brand specializing in handcrafted body scrubs and body butters. Her creativity and determination shine through in every endeavor she pursues.

Above all, Blue is a devoted mother to an extraordinary daughter who has followed in her footsteps as both an author and entrepreneur, continuing a legacy of creativity and resilience. Stay tuned for more inspiring works from Blue Kendria Berry in the near future!

Author - Blue Kendria Berry .

Find additional resources and information about Blue Kendria Berry at

Website - www.beautifulkreations.shop

Facebook - @Blue Kendria

Tiktok - @Blue_Kendria

Instagram - @beautifulkreationsllc

www.ingramcontent.com/pod-product-compliance
Lightning Source LLC
LaVergne TN
LVHW072050060526
838201LV00029B/324/J